Papa Andrea's

SICILIAN TABLE

Papa Andrea's

SICILIAN TABLE

⚜

Recipes From a
Sicilian Chef
As Remembered by
His Grandson

⚜

VINCENT SCHIAVELLI

A Citadel Press Book
Published by Carol Publishing Group

Carol Publishing Group Edition, 1995

Copyright © 1993 by Vincent Schiavelli
All rights reserved.
No part of this book may be reproduced in any form,
except by a newspaper or magazine reviewer who wishes to quote
brief passages in connection with a review.

A Citadel Press Book
Published by Carol Publishing Group

Citadel Press is a registered trademark of Carol Communications, Inc.
Editorial Offices: 600 Madison Avenue, New York, N.Y. 10022
Sales and Distribution Offices: 120 Enterprise Avenue, Secaucus, N.J. 07094
In Canada: Canadian Manda Group,
One Atlantic Avenue, Suite 105, Toronto, Ontario, M6K 3E7
Queries regarding rights and permissions should be addressed to
Carol Publishing Group,
600 Madison Avenue, New York, N.Y. 10022

Carol Publishing Group books are available at special discounts for bulk purchases,
for sales promotion, fund-raising, or educational purposes. Special editions can be created to specifications.
For details, contact: Special Sales Department, Carol Publishing Group,
120 Enterprise Avenue, Secaucus, N.J. 07094

Art Direction: Louise Fili
Design: Leah Lococo
Typesetting: Cheryl Knippenberg
Illustrations: Paolo Guidotti

Manufactured in the United States of America
10 9 8 7 6 5 4 3 2 1

Library of Congress Cataloging-in-Publication Data
Schiavelli, Vincent.
Papa Andrea's Sicilian Table: recipes from a Sicilian chef as
remembered by his grandson / by Vincent Schiavelli.
p. cm.
"A Citadel Press book."
ISBN 0-8065-1709-3 (pbk)
1. Cookery, Italian–Sicilian style. I Title.
TX723.2.S55S35 1993
641.59458–dc20   95-19790
                                         CIP

 FOR MY GRANDFATHER

MAESTRO ANDREA COCO (1872–1968)

WHO WAS THE FIRST TO TEACH

ME OF THE MAGIC OF LIFE

CONTENTS

Contents

Contents

Contents

Contents

Contents

☙

☙

☙

$\mathcal{C}$ ontents

I Pezzi Duri 167

(Molded Frozen Desserts)

⚜

INTRODUCTION

This cookbook contains authentic recipes from the northern mountains of Sicily as they were taught to me by my grandfather, Andrea Coco, master chef to the baron Rampolla in that region at the turn of the twentieth century. Sicilian food is divided into two basic categories: *a cucina povera*, the cuisine of the poor, and *'a cucina ricca*, the cuisine of the rich. The division is based on local abundance or scarcity of ingredients and the financial ability to import them from other regions of Sicily or even from the mainland. By selecting a menu composed of both categories for the same meal, as my grandfather Papa Andrea often did, the counterpoint between simple, frank flavors and subtle, complex ones provides a truly magnificent array of flavor. But I am moving ahead of my story. Let me begin at its beginning.

On October 30, 1872, Andrea Coco was born in a small town named Isnello in the Madonie, a mountain range in northern Sicily. His parents were *cuntadini*, peasant farmers. Their work was labor intensive, involving the farming of terraced gardens in the hot Sicilian sun. Today one still sees these workers with their strong, leathery faces walking home to Isnello in the evening carrying their hoes and scythes on their shoulders.

As a boy, Andrea was an intelligent lad with the devil in his eye. He often found himself in trouble for some mischief or other. One story he told me was how, as an altar boy, he put vinegar in the cruet for mass instead of wine. It was for a high mass sung in Latin. The priest drank it at the most solemn part of the service and registered the unmistakable look of someone who has just drunk vinegar. Without dropping a note, he sang, not the liturgy, but to Andrea in perfect Gregorian chant in Sicilian, "So it has come to this! You give me vinegar! When we go back to the sacristy we are going to have a little chat!" Andrea responded in the same language and meter, "If you can find me!" and left. The parishioners didn't notice the variation.

When he was sixteen Andrea left Isnello and journeyed by foot to a city long the seat of power and culture of the region—Polizzi Generosa, a beautiful city strategically placed on a mountaintop 4,000 feet above sea level. The wide promenades overlooking expansive vistas of the olive groves and hazelnut trees of the baronial estates, the magnificent Arab-Norman architecture and Spanish baroque churches, the aristocratic inhabitants dressed in their fine clothes strolling or riding in well-appointed carriages, filled Andrea, he told me, with the greatest excitement. Polizzi Generosa predates ancient Rome. Its name is rooted in the ancient Greek for city, *polis.* Later the Romans built roads, fortifications, and country villas in the area. The earliest existing written record of Polizzi is from the Byzantines, set down in 880. The record makes reference to a fortress built there by them a century earlier. Polizzi was conquered by Saracens from North Africa in 882 and remained under Arab rule until the Norman conquest of the Madonie Mountains in 1071. A mosque from the Arab period still exists, reconsecrated as a Roman Catholic church during the Norman occupation. Although Arab rule lasted for only 181 years, the influence of the Levant was present for centuries before and after its domination of the area. The refinement of this culture through what Europe called its Dark and Middle Ages has had a profound effect on the customs, language, and cuisine of Polizzi as well as on most of Sicily.

In 1234 Federico II, the great Norman king of Sicily, visited Polizzi. He was so moved by the generous hospitality he encountered during his sojourn there that he decreed henceforth it would be a city called Polizzi "la Generosa." As a result of this decree, Polizzi Generosa was freed from baronial ownership and given a seat in the Sicilian parliament of the time. Under its own coat of arms—a golden field with seven roses surmounted by the imperial eagle—it flourished and prospered through the next seven centuries despite an endless wave of conquerors. France, Austria, and Spain, to name three of the most prominent, conquered and occupied Polizzi and left behind elements of their cultures and cuisines. Not until the unification of Italy under the House of Savoy in 1860 did Polizzi begin its decline. Its position no longer of strategic importance, it lost its place to other, more accessible cities. Corrupt rule, high taxes, and the growing inviability of ancient social and economic systems caused mass immigration. By the first part of the twentieth century it was but a shadow of its former glory. Today Polizzi Generosa is a small city of 5,000. It remains extremely beautiful, proud, and gracious. There is a strong sense of its rich history from another age.

It was to this place in its last flowering that Andrea Coco arrived in 1888. He was apprenticed to a goldsmith, but quickly realized that this trade, although extremely lucrative, did not capture his heart. He joined the cavalry but realized after a brief hitch that this life was also not for him. After this experience he made a living at odd jobs. Through a friend he obtained work for a week in the kitchen of one of the baronial estates that was preparing a grand wedding feast for the baron's youngest daughter. This kitchen was ruled by Cologero Vilardi, a famous cook and pastry chef of the region, who was known to be what is called a *monzú*. At the beginning of the nineteenth century it became fashionable among the aristocracy of Sicily to import French chefs (who had recently become unemployed because of the Revolution). Also, they would send their Sicilian chefs to France to learn French methods. These techniques were applied to Sicilian cuisine. When the chefs returned to Sicily they were called monsieur at first, but quickly became known as *monzú*, a Sicilian adaptation of the French word. The *monzú* were renowned for their great culinary abilities, volatile temperaments, and playful cunning in guarding their secrets. After a time these chefs were no longer sent to France, but the tradition continued through a system of apprenticeship.

Andrea Coco (top row, right) during his apprenticeship to Cologero Vilardi (top row, second from left). Polizzi Generosa, c. 1891

My grandfather told me that he immediately became enraptured by the master's artistry in the kitchen. He carefully watched all of his moves. Andrea convinced Maestro Cologero to take him as an apprentice. He was a good student and in time became a master himself, a *monzú*. By this time he was cooking in the service of a powerful, titled family of Polizzi named Rampolla. He soon became head chef for the baron, an honored lifetime position.

15

In what little free time he had, Andrea played the role of the young man about town. Handsome, with red hair, clear eyes, and an elaborate mustache, he rode his horse, Lola, through the streets of Polizzi, and was admired and sought after by young ladies who flirted with him shamelessly from the safety of their balconies. One day one of the young ladies was especially thrilled to see him. He had been ill with a chest cold; nothing serious, but it had laid him up for a couple of weeks. In an effort to make a big show of her concern for his health, amid thankyous to all the saints in heaven and crocodile tears of joy she tossed him some lire. She instructed him to go to the church and light a candle at a statue of the Virgin in thanks for restoring him to good health. Andrea took the money, but instead of going to church he went to a baker to buy hard biscuits for his horse and to the cigar store for himself. A short while later, he was riding down her street, puffing away on his cigar. The young lady called down to him, "Andrea, did you light it?" "Oh yes," he said, "and how it's burning!"

The world was changing, however; changing even in this small city in the Sicilian mountains. The old order was beginning to crack. Partly out of a desire to be free of the bonds of servitude and mostly out of a desire for adventure, Andrea Coco, at the age of twenty-nine, booked passage to America.

Every detail of my grandfather Andrea's first few days in New York City in 1901 was engraved on his memory. Sixty years later he could recall with startling accuracy the address of the restaurant where he ate his first meal in America, where he spent his first night, and how he searched for and found a cousin who had emigrated earlier. It was through this cousin that he found work in an Italian restaurant. This experience opened his eyes to the realities of the American restaurant business of the time. The hot, claustrophobic kitchen was a far cry from the cook house set in an olive grove on a baronial estate. He found the policies regarding the freshness and quality of the food not up to his rigid standards. His artistry and accomplishments as *monzú* meant nothing in this new world. So he soon left the food business, never to return, and worked for the next fifty years as a buyer for a wholesale fruit market in Brooklyn.

Several years passed after this move, and Andrea was courting a young woman; they were about to be engaged. One evening she mentioned in passing that she had heard that a close acquaintance of his from Polizzi was in Brooklyn with two of his daughters. It was Maestro Cologero Vilardi, his former teacher. Andrea remembered one of his daughters, Carolina, vividly. When last they

Andrea Coco and Carolin Vilardi on the occasion of their engagement.
Brooklyn, September 27, 1905

had met, she was a schoolgirl of twelve preparing herself to eventually enter the normal school in Polizzi. Even though she was a child at that time, Andrea was struck by Carolina's goodness, intelligence, and beauty. When Andrea ascertained that one of the daughters accompanying the Maestro was indeed Carolina, he broke off his relationship with his girlfriend. He told me he knew without even seeing her that the girl Carolina must have grown into the woman whose hand he would pursue in marriage.

Andrea's and Carolina's courtship was romantic, intense—and chaperoned. When he would visit her, they would converse in the constant presence of her father and her sister. Toward the end of the evening, Carolina would sweep the floor, a ruse designed to gather a neatly folded love letter which he would drop to the floor by his feet. She would place her letter to him in the pocket of his overcoat. These letters were written in Sicilian, hers on fine stationery in a sure, delicate, educated hand; his in more of a scrawl, sometimes on the letterhead of the fruit market laden with the engravings of bananas and crates of California fruit. One of Andrea's letters to Carolina reads like this:

My Life's Breath

Last night after I left your house I reached into my pocket and found a sweet little note. But I cannot imagine who put it there, as there was no signature. Why do you deny me the pleasure of seeing your name? Do you not know that you are the caretaker of my heart?

Take many hot kisses and affectionate embraces from he who is unforgettably yours,

Andrea

Andrea, at thirty-three, and Carolina, at twenty-three, were married on April 15, 1906. Until her death in 1960, even after more than fifty years of marriage, there was still ardent passion in their eyes when they looked at each other.

As time passed, Andrea and Carolina raised a family. Most of Carolina's relatives emigrated from Polizzi Generosa. Over the years, Andrea became paterfamilias to a large group of children, grandchildren, nieces, nephews, cousins, and in-laws. It seemed the whole world called him Papa Andrea.

One of their daughters is my mother. After my father's sudden death when I was three years old, my mother and I moved in with my grandparents. I grew up and lived in the same household as my two unmarried aunts, my grandmother, and my grandfather Papa Andrea. I knew him through his eighties and nineties. He remained physically strong well into his ninety-sixth year and mentally clear to the last. Even though we were in Brooklyn, not Sicily, our household was closer to Polizzi Generosa than to the America of "Leave It to Beaver" or "Father Knows Best."

As a boy, I would do my homework at one end of the kitchen table while Papa Andrea prepared dinner at the other. I loved to watch his neat, methodical approach to cooking: his meatballs or potato croquettes or arancini lined up in straight rows like soldiers on waxed paper, his chopped onions or mushrooms piled in exact-sized pieces on the cutting board, his salads presented in beautiful arrangements on oval platters, his sauces delicate and exquisite. When my work was finished he answered all my questions about the food. Often Papa Andrea would tell me stories. Some of these were about a wondrous land called Sicily, a place where watermelons were round and small and artichokes were so tender they could be eaten whole. Others were about life on the baronial estate or his early times in New York. He told me these stories over and over, hardly varying a word. I heard them each time as if it were the first. They taught me important lessons on how to be a man and a gentleman in a hostile world. How to be a person unafraid of emotion, beauty, or tenderness. To show strength and self-discipline in one's commitments and responsibilities. To have patience and perseverance in all endeavors. And above all, to always show respect for everyone. He would often recite the Sicilian proverb *"U rispettu è misuratu cui purtu l'avu purtatu."* (Respect is measured. He who brings it has it brought back to him.) Papa Andrea believed that even if respect was not reciprocated, one should always do the honorable thing.

Cologero Vilardi (left) and Andrea Coco (right), Brooklyn, Septembe, 27 ,1905

Papa Andrea's wit, sense of humor, and playful teasing were irrepressible. One frozen day in February during his ninety-fourth year he slipped and fell on the ice at six a.m. while at the corner candy store to buy the morning newspapers. That evening the candy store's owner alerted one of my aunts of this event as she returned home from work. With great concern she asked him, "Papa. Did you fall on the ice this morning?" He responded in the affirmative with a solemnness matching hers. "What did you do?" she questioned further. "I got up," he said, adding a wry little smile.

Whenever anyone asked Papa Andrea for a recipe, he would give it freely, but always leave something out. After they tried it and would report that the dish simply didn't taste like his, he always said, "What a mystery. But listen, if you ever want to eat that, come here and I will be happy to prepare it for you." My grandfather was very protective of his recipes, not sharing his secrets, a common attitude in the tradition of the *monzú*. With me, however, he shared them all. It seems he chose to pass the tradition to me, an honor for which I remain eternally grateful.

Papa Andrea was an outspoken anti-cleric. He had little use for organized religion, a fact which deeply troubled his wife and daughters. They would constantly entreat him to return to the Church. He would cheerfully explain his reasons with this story. One Good Friday the baron with his entourage, including the bishop, went for a picnic in the country. The table was being set. The cold buffet, which was meatless—conforming to the laws of the Church regarding this holy day—was being laid out. The bishop told my grandfather he was craving rabbit and asked him to send someone to catch a colony of rabbits for lunch. Papa Andrea said, "Excuse me, Your Excellency, but it is Good Friday." The bishop responded, "Good Friday! Good Friday? My son, there is no Good Friday in the country."

A story which my grandfather told me only once was about the death of his own grandfather. When Papa Andrea was six, he accompanied his grandfather into the orchard to pick pears. The old man climbed the tree to get the high, ripe ones and told his young grandson to shake the tree. My grandfather's grandfather suffered a heart attack and fell to the ground. He was dead. Some eighty years later, as my grandfather told me this story, his eyes filled up with tears. "I thought he was asleep. I was only a little boy. I didn't know. I just sat on the ground and ate pears." As the years pass I have a growing understanding of his deep emotional connection to this grandfather and his continued sense of loss over his passing.

Although Papa Andrea did not pursue a cooking career in America, he cooked every day for the family. Sunday dinner was a banquet for at least eighteen people. My aunts and uncles and cousins would arrive at about one o'clock. As young children, we ate first and then were sent off to play. Papa Andrea would cut the pasta boxes into crenelated castles with his pocket knife. The lids became chairs and, below the plastic window, the mighty gates. There were no people for these castles. The aristocrats and noblemen were long ago and far away. As we children grew older we ate with the adults but at our own table, a tradition we insisted upon well into our twenties.

When the pasta was served, one of my aunts, an ample woman, would always ask for a small portion in her best, school-learned Italian, a language as quaint and foreign to Papa Andrea as English. "Only two strands of pasta for me." Papa Andrea would respond literally by ceremoniously placing two strands of pasta in a pasta bowl with a dribble of tomato sauce and a pinch of grated cheese. Everyone, and especially my aunt, would laugh at the ridiculous sight of these two lonely strands in the middle of a glistening white bowl. "Oh Papa," she would smile." But isn't that what you asked for?" he would question in mock bewilderment. And then, "All right. Leave it to me," as he filled her bowl, which made her very happy. This ritual was repeated in exactly the same way every Sunday. Course after course would follow, amid jokes, gossip, and lively conversation on every topic.

After dinner we children would gather around Papa Andrea who, with his trusty pocket knife, would peel each of us an orange, magically fashioning the peel into eyeglasses, front and sides all in one piece. Sometimes we would perform for the adults—my cousin Caroline with her beautiful voice, my cousin Kenny on his violin, and me portraying some role for which I was impossibly too young. Papa Andrea would watch beaming, very proud.

Perhaps these experiences are not unlike those of other Sicilian families. The difference in ours was that the centerpiece of our Sunday table in this working class Brooklyn apartment was the food of Maestro Andrea Coco, *monzù* to the Baron Rampolla of Polizzi Generosa.

Over the years, I have visited Sicily and learned more about Sicilian cuisine. Papa Andrea's recipes are not only a part of this 2,500-year-old tradition, but his subtle and refined interpretation of traditional dishes has set for him an important place at the table of the *monzù*, the master chefs of Sicily.

The recipes in this book are from the hands and the spirit of Papa Andrea. I trust they will delight you as they have so many others for the past hundred years.

'A CUCINA POVERA

(The Cuisine of the Poor)

In Sicily, there is an early spring vegetable stew named "'a Frittedda." While I was in Polizzi Generosa, I discussed its ingredients with an expert on the local cuisine. When I told him that we always put prosciutto in it and ate it hot, he said, "Here, we put vinegar and eat it cold. We don't make prosciutto here, but if you are rich, you can do whatever you like."

'A FRITTEDDA

Frittedda is a stew of artichokes, fava beans, peas, and asparagus flavored with fennel and prosciutto. It is eaten in the early spring when these vegetables first appear, as a testament to the earth in renewal.

FOR SIX SERVINGS

2½ pounds baby artichokes, about 3 inches long	2 ounces prosciutto
	¼ cup extra virgin olive oil
1½ pounds fava beans	black pepper
1¼ asparagus	2 lemons
1 pound sweet peas	sea salt
¼ pound fennel, leaves and stems	

To prepare the artichokes, set up a bowl of water with the juice and rind of one of the lemons. Pass a knife through the other lemon prior to each cut to prevent the artichoke from turning black. Cut off ½ inch from the top of the artichoke. Peel away the outer leaves to the place at which the leaves are pale green and thinner. Cut off the stem, cut the artichoke in half, and place it in the bowl of lemon and water. This seems like a monumental task, but after the first few, it moves along very quickly. Add the juice and rind of the second lemon to the bowl and let the artichokes soak in it until cooking time.

In a separate bowl, shell the fava beans and peas. Cut off the tough ends of the asparagus and discard. Cut the asparagus in 1¼ inch lengths. Clean the fennel tops, remove the thick stems, and chop the rest fine. Chop the prosciutto in small dice (cubes).

Heat the olive oil and prosciutto in a heavy pot on medium heat. When the prosciutto begins to cook, turn down the heat and add the drained artichokes. Turn them to distribute the fat. Cover and cook for 10 minutes. If they begin to stick, add a little water.

After the 10 minutes, add all the other vegetables, fennel, salt, and pepper.

Stir to mix everything together well. Cover and cook on low heat for about 30 minutes. Stir from time to time, adding a little water if necessary, but when it is ready there should be very little liquid remaining. Serve this dish hot, accompanied with good bread and a cheese such as provolone, caciocavalo, or primosale.

&

MINESTRA 'I LINTICCHI
(Lentil Soup)

FOR FOUR SERVINGS

1¼ cups lentils, soaked in
   cold water for 2 hours

2 ounces pancetta

2 tablespoons extra virgin olive oil

1 medium-sized onion, sliced thin

3 cloves garlic, chopped

3 ribs celery, sliced thin

2 sprigs mint, chopped

2 quarts hot water

1 large bunch Italian parsley, chopped

sea salt

black pepper

Place the olive oil and onion in a four-quart pot on the stove. Turn on the heat to medium and sauté the onion until clear. Do not allow it to brown in any way. Add the pancetta, cut in small dice, celery, and garlic. Continue to sauté for five minutes. Add the soaked, drained lentils and gently turn them in the pot until they absorb all the fat. Add the mint and black pepper, pour in the hot water, and add parsley and salt.

Cook at medium heat with the cover askew for 1¼ hours. Allow the soup to boil freely. Stir it to prevent burning and sticking.

The result will be a thick, hearty soup great on a cold day.

L'OVA 'NCAMISSA
(Egg-in-a-Shirt Soup)

This wonderful, fast peasant favorite has the ability to warm in the winter and refresh in the summer.

FOR TWO SERVINGS

1 potato	sea salt
¼ cup extra virgin olive oil	black pepper
2 eggs	grated Locatelli or Pecorino cheese
4 sprigs Italian parsley, chopped	

Peel and dice the potato, cook it in about 3 cups of water with the olive oil and the salt. When the potato is cooked, break in the eggs one at a time, being careful not to break the yolks. Poach the eggs in the broth until the white is cooked and the yolks are still runny. Fish the eggs gently out of the broth, placing one in each bowl. Divide the remaining contents of the pot, sprinkle with parsley, black pepper, and grated cheese. Break the yolks in the bowl before eating.

If you are preparing this for a large group, and the pot seems too crowded for all the eggs, you can poach the eggs in some of the broth in a different pot.

L'OVA BRUDUCHIDDU
(Egg in a Light Broth)

The ingredients are the same as for L'Ova 'Ncamissa, but instead of poaching the eggs, beat them before adding them to the broth. Continue to beat them while cooking, until they are *strachata* which is to say, shredded.

If the eggs break while making L'Ova 'Ncamissa, you can always make l'ova bruduchiddi instead, and you don't have to tell anyone.

FROCIA 'I CIPPUDDI
(Sicilian-Style Onion Omelet)

When I was eight years old, the first thing my grandfather Papa Andrea taught me to cook was this Sicilian-style omelet with onion. At first I was permitted to cut the onion only in half. He would chop it. I could grate the cheese from a very large piece, beat the eggs, and gently pour them into the pan under his loving, watchful eye. He, of course, would turn it in the pan. As we ate our creation, we took pride in our delicious, simple but masterful luncheon.

As a teenager I became quite accomplished in the preparation of a *frocia*—except when my grandfather was in the room. He would watch me, expressionless, warning me in grave tones—the onion was about to burn, the frocia would break when I tried to turn it. Sure enough, under his gaze tragedy would always befall my efforts. At this he would bellow out a great laugh, knowing that he had gotten me.

FOR ONE SERVING

2 eggs

3 tablespoons locatelli or imported
   pecorino cheese, grated

1 teaspoon milk

2 sprigs Italian parsley, chopped

½ medium onion, chopped fine
   (about ¼ cup)

2 tablespoons extra virgin olive oil

black pepper

Thoroughly beat together the eggs, milk, grated cheese, parsley, and black pepper with a fork.

Place the onion and olive oil in a well-cured 6-inch omelet pan. Turn on the heat to medium and sauté the onion until clear. Do not allow it to brown in any way.

Pour in the egg mixture. Use a fork to make sure the onion is well distributed but keep it a little in from the edges of the egg in the pan.

When the side facing the pan achieves a deep golden brown, carefully turn it over. Cook the other side to the same color. Serve immediately, accompanied with bread and olives.

FROCIA 'I PATATI

(Sicilian-Style Potato Omelet)

This large frocia is cooked in a slightly different way than the previous ones. Papa Andrea would prepare double this recipe in a 12-inch skillet.

FOR FOUR SERVINGS

³/₄ pound white potatoes, peeled, cut, and boiled

4 anchovies, chopped

2 tablespoons butter

³/₄ cup milk

¹/₄ cup cream

6 eggs, beaten

¹/₂ cup locatelli or imported pecorino cheese, grated

4 sprigs Italian parsley, chopped

2 tablespoons extra virgin olive oil

sea salt

black pepper

When the potatoes are cooked, drain and immediately add the anchovies and butter. Mash into a smooth puree. Add the milk and cream.

Now grate the cheese and chop the parsley. Beat the eggs very well in a separate bowl.

When the potato mixture has cooled enough so as not to cook the beaten eggs, add them as well as the grated cheese, parsley, and black pepper. Salt if necessary. The mixture will be smooth, having the consistency of batter.

Place a heavy, well-cured 9-inch skillet on the stove. Pour in the olive oil. Turn on the heat to medium. When the oil is nearly smoking, place the egg mixture in the pan. Be sure it is distributed evenly. Turn down the heat to very low and cook the frocia slowly for about half an hour until it is a rich golden brown on the bottom side. You can peek at it by gently lifting an edge with a spatula. Toward the end of this time, make certain it has not stuck to the pan by twisting the pan back and forth.

The traditional way of cooking the top side of this type of frocia is to turn it over onto a plate, then slide it off the plate back into the pan. I have found, however, that an easier method is not to turn it at all, but to simply place the pan in the broiler with the rack set at the greatest distance from the flame. If the handle of your pan is plastic, leave the door open with the handle sticking out so it doesn't melt. Cook it in this manner for only a few minutes and check it often, as it can easily burn.

This frocia may be served hot or at room temperature.

FROCIA 'I SPARACI
(Sicilian-Style Asparagus Omelet)

FOR FOUR SERVINGS

1 pound asparagus, the thickest
available

½ clove garlic, peeled

6 eggs

1 cup locatelli or imported
pecorino cheese, grated

2 tablespoons extra virgin olive oil

sea salt

black pepper

Trim the asparagus of their woody ends. Steam them with the half clove of garlic in the steaming water for about 12 minutes or until tender, but firm. The best way to steam asparagus is tied in bundles standing with the bottom inch submerged in water. This will allow the thick end to cook at the same rate as the top. There are pots especially designed for this purpose. If you do not have one of these, perhaps lurking somewhere in your kitchen is a percolator coffeepot. This will serve very well with the innards removed and a piece of aluminum foil placed over the spout.

When the asparagus stalks are cooked, lift them out of the pot and snip open the bundles. Lightly salt and reserve the asparagus until ready for use.

Beat the eggs very well with the grated cheese and black pepper.

Place a heavy, well-cured 9-inch skillet on the stove. Pour in the olive oil. Turn on the heat to medium, and when it is hot, add the asparagus. Turn them in the oil for a minute or two. Do not allow them to brown in any way. Arrange the asparagus in one layer in the pan. Use a fork and knife or a spatula to cut pieces to fit.

Pour in the egg mixture, turn down the heat very low, and cook the frocia using the same method as for Frocia 'i Patati. This one, however, will take less time to cook.

Serve hot. This recipe may also be doubled and cooked in a 12-inch skillet.

I CUDURUNA

$\mathscr{I}$n the Madonie, a mountain range in northern Sicily, there is a pensione named L'Università della Moritore. Its translation is "Bricklayer's University." Thinking this an odd name for an inn, I asked the owner what it meant. He said, "I have been building this place for ten years, and for me it has been a university."

L'Università della Moritore is famous for its local rustic cuisine. One weekend, there were big doings. Saturday night, it played host to a party of twelve from Palermo. They had come to eat Testa di Vitello, stewed veal head served cold with several simple sauces. One can eat this same dish at Fouquet's in Paris. Sunday, there was scheduled a party of twenty, also from Palermo, for lunch. Sunday evening, there was to be a local family's christening party of a hundred.

The owner, Santo Lipani, his employee Domenico, and a third man hired especially for these occasions, Turiddu, worked in the kitchen from Thursday morning on preparing for the christening feast. Sunday morning was time to bake the bread. The process began at dawn.

The bread dough was made in an ancient trough carved out of a single log. The bakers used their fists as dough hooks to mix and knead the dough. The dough was then covered and kept in a warm place for three hours to rise. In the meantime, a wood fire was built in a large outdoor brick oven. It was a cold, damp, rainy November morning in the mountains. We huddled around the warming oven and told stories and drank coffee. At 8:30 in the morning, four of the luncheon guests from Palermo arrived, hoping to spend the day in the country. They were disappointed to find it raining and joined us around the oven.

After the first rising, small oval loaves were quickly formed and placed on a floured wooden board. They were beautiful, yellow from the semolina flour, and filled with the sweet yeasty smell of bread dough. The loaves were covered for the second rising. Turiddu sensed these coverings were not sufficient to keep the dough warm, and lent his coat to the operation. The second rising was shorter, about 40 minutes. During this time the oven, hot by now, was prepared. The embers were pushed to the sides of the oven, the floor meticulously cleaned with a long-handled metal scraper. A bucket of embers was removed and kept nearby. A cross was cut on the top of each loaf to ward off the evil eye, and with a prayer, they were arranged on the oven floor. The iron door of the oven was hooked into place and the embers were used to seal it. It was as if we were firing pottery.

Someone noticed that three of the loaves were left out. Santo, who was in charge of loading, assured us there was no more room anyway. Domenico, with a look of glee on his face, took the loaves into the kitchen. He flattened the loaves, cut the dough in triangular pieces, and fried them in a fruity, extra virgin olive oil from the area. He brought the fried dough out to us, still at our vigil around the oven, and we ate it dipped in sugar. One lady from Palermo ate hers with salt. Santo, Domenico, and Turiddu shrugged and laughed as if to say there was no accounting for the strange ways of folks from the big city. They assured us all that the only way to eat cuduruna was dipped in sugar.

Incidentally, the bread was the best I'd ever tasted. We ate it, first, hot from the oven, split, moistened with olive oil and seasoned with black pepper. When it was cooled, it accompanied lunch, and then dinner. Finally, we ate it, four days later, as toast with jam for breakfast.

❧

PANI 'I CASA
(Semolina Bread)

In the mountains of Sicily, bread is made from semolina flour—flour made from the same yellow, hard durum wheat as pasta, but ground much finer, having the consistency of flour as we know it.

Since most of us do not have a brick oven at our disposal, it is advisable to use a baking stone or line the oven with unglazed terra cotta tiles. If you obtain your tiles from a flooring company and they are not specifically designed for baking, the lime must be removed. Soak the tiles in water for forty-eight hours. When they are dry, dust the white powder from the surface. Fit the tiles in your oven, and give them a good thirty minutes of preheating before use. Do not attempt to remove them from the oven until they are cool, as the rapid change in temperature may cause them to crack. If anything ever sticks or burns onto the tiles, they can be cleaned dry with fine sandpaper.

FOR EACH LOAF

About 3 cups semolina flour

3/4 heaping teaspoon salt

1 1/2 teaspoons dry active yeast

3/4 teaspoon sugar

1 to 1 1/2 cups hand-hot water

1 1/2 tablespoons extra virgin olive oil

coarse semolina for dusting

Mix the yeast and sugar together in a warmed glass. Add some of the water and mix with a wooden spoon. Let stand for 10 minutes until the yeast is foamy and crackling. Meanwhile, mix the flour and salt together in a large wooden or heated bowl. When the yeast is ready, mix it in. Mix in the olive oil and water. Continue mixing until it forms a ball. If it is too loose or sticky, add a bit more flour; if too dry, add more water. Knead the dough for 10 minutes after a ball is formed.

Lightly flour the inside of a bowl, place the dough ball in it, cut a cross on top, and dust it with flour. Cover the bowl and set it in a warm place for three hours, until the dough's volume has doubled.

After the first rising, gently knock down (pound) the dough by kneading for a couple of seconds. Shape the dough into an oval loaf. Dust a work surface with coarse semolina and place the loaf on it. Dust the top of the loaf with fine flour and let it rise for about 40 minutes. Depending on temperature, it may be necessary to cover the loaf.

Meanwhile, place the tiles on a rack in the center of the oven and preheat at 450° for 30 minutes.

When the loaf has completed the second rising, cut a cross on the top of it, about 1 inch deep. Slip the loaf onto a paddle dusted with course semolina and slide it into the oven. Bake at 450° for 10 minutes, then reduce the heat to 425° and continue baking for 45 minutes longer.

If you need more bread, increase this recipe in exact proportions.

⚓

SCHIACHATA 'I ANCIOVI
(Pizza With Anchovies)

This Sicilian-style pizza, topped only with anchovies, is delicious by itself or as an accompaniment to a cooked leafy green vegetable.

THE RECIPE GIVEN HERE IS FOR ONE

10-INCH X 16-INCH PAN PIZZA.

Prepare one recipe of Pani 'i Casa up to the end of the first rising. Meanwhile, preheat the oven to 450°.

Grease a 10-inch x 16-inch oven pan with olive oil. Stretch the dough to fit into the pan. Arrange anchovies on top of the dough. Drizzle the olive oil from the tin of anchovies over the top. Place in the center of the oven and immediately turn down the heat to 400°. Bake for 15 to 20 minutes and serve very hot.

SFINCIUNI CUNZATU
CU BROCCULEDDU E RICOTTA

(Sfinciuni Filled With Broccoli and Ricotta)

Sfinciuni is a closed Sicilian pizza. The crust is made of the same dough as Pani 'i Casa, but it is rolled thin. The filling is bountiful. There are many different fillings used. I have included two here that I enjoy.

FOR SIX SERVINGS

DOUGH

2 cups semolina flour	1 tablespoon extra virgin olive oil
1 heaping teaspoon sea salt	1 cup hand-hot water
1 teaspoon dry active yeast	coarse semolina for dusting
½ teaspoon sugar	

FILLING

1 pound homemade ricotta or 1½ pounds store-bought ricotta (see method under "Cannoli")	4 tablespoons extra virgin olive oil
	2 tablespoons bread crumbs
	nutmeg
	black pepper
1 pound broccoli	sea salt

Prepare the dough as for Pani 'i Casa up to the end of the first rising in the proportions listed above. Meanwhile, preheat the oven with the tiles for half an hour before baking to 425°, and prepare the filling with enough time for it to cool to room temperature.

To prepare the filling, first steam the broccoli until it is three-quarters cooked. Chop it in small pieces and sauté it in 2 tablespoons olive oil until tender. Add salt and a few scrapes of nutmeg. Remove from the pan and let it cool to room temperature.

When the dough has completed its first rising, divide it in half and roll it into two circles, about 12 inches in diameter, one slightly larger than the other. Place the larger circle on a paddle dusted with coarse semolina and spread with 1 tablespoon of olive oil and 1 tablespoon of bread crumbs. Bring these ingredients ³/₄-inch from the edge. Spread the ricotta and then the broccoli on top in the same way. Sprinkle with 1 tablespoon olive oil and 1 tablespoon bread crumbs. Place the smaller circle on top and roll the edges of both circles together, forming a tight seal. Brush the top crust with water and slide it into the oven. Bake for 20 to 25 minutes, or until the crust is golden brown. Let it rest for 10 minutes before serving.

⚜

SFINCIUNI CUNZATU CU CARNI E CACCIU
(Sfinciuni Filled With Meat and Cheese)

FOR SIX SERVINGS

1 recipe of dough for Sfinciuni

1 medium onion, chopped fine

1 pound lean ground pork

2 tablespoons fennel seeds

2 tablespoons tomato paste

$\frac{1}{2}$ cup dry white wine

$\frac{1}{2}$ pound caciocavalo
   or imported provolone cheese,
   cut in small dice (cubes)

$\frac{1}{2}$ pound cooked ham,
   not smoked, cut in
   small dice (cubes)

6 very ripe Roma
   or Italian plum tomatoes

2 tablespoons bread crumbs

3 tablespoons extra virgin olive oil

Sauté the onion in 2 tablespoons of the olive oil until golden brown; do not let it burn. Add the pork and cook it until it is well done. Dissolve the tomato paste in the white wine and add, along with the fennel seeds, a generous amount of black pepper with a scarce amount of salt. Let it cook together for another couple of minutes until most of the liquid is evaporated. When cooled, add the ham and cheese.

Prepare and roll out the dough in the same way as for the other Sfinciuni in this book: place 1 tablespoon of bread crumbs on the bottom of the crust to ¾ of an inch from the edge. Spread the meat and cheese mixture in the same way. Cover the mixture with thin slices of tomato, one tablespoon of bread crumbs, and olive oil before putting the top crust in place. Bake in the same way as the other Sfinciuni, also allowing 10 minutes before serving.

'A PIZZA FRITTA
(Fried Pizza)

This pizza takes 20 minutes to prepare and cook. Although it is wonderfully simple it never ceases to delight the palate and the eye.

Sift together 1 cup of unbleached flour, 1 teaspoon of baking powder, and ½ teaspoon of salt. Add enough water to form dough. Cover, and while it is resting, prepare the topping. Use whatever good things are lurking in your refrigerator in small quantities: a bit of cheese, fresh tomato and basil, or some anchovies perhaps. I once used the fish and onion from a small amount of leftover fish soup, and it was quite good.

Roll out the dough to 9 inches in diameter. Heat a good ½ inch of extra virgin olive oil in a 9-inch skillet until it is almost smoking. Slip in the dough, turn down the heat to low, and cook for about 2 minutes. Turn it over, arrange the topping, cover the pan, and cook until the topping is hot or melted. Lift the pizza out of the pan, leaving behind all the oil, and serve immediately.

⚓

PASTA E PISEDDI
(Pasta With Peas)

FOR FOUR SERVINGS

³/₄ pound peas	4 scrapes nutmeg
1 pound ditalini or tubetti pasta	sea salt
⅓ medium onion, chopped very fine	black pepper
⅓ to ½ cup extra virgin olive oil	grated locatelli or pecorino cheese

Put up a large pot of water with salt and a little olive oil in which to cook the pasta. Chop the onion and place it with ³/₄ cup water and a little salt in a small saucepan. Simmer covered on low heat. When the pasta water boils, put in the pasta and then add the peas, olive oil, nutmeg, and black pepper to the small saucepan. Cook the peas covered, for about five minutes, until they are cooked. Toss with the pasta in a heated bowl and serve with grated cheese.

Pasta e Piseddi is often served very soupy. In order to allow for this option, reserve some of the water in which the pasta was cooked and add it back to the dish. Adjust the olive oil and the salt. The right "soupiness" for me is achieved by not draining the pasta too thoroughly.

PASTA AGGHIU OGGHIU
(Pasta With Garlic and Oil)

FOR FOUR SERVINGS

1 pound linguini pasta	3 sprigs Italian parsley, chopped
5 cloves garlic, chopped very fine	sea salt
½ cup extra virgin olive oil	black pepper
crushed red pepper to taste	toasted bread crumbs

While the linguini is cooking, place the chopped garlic, red pepper, and parsley in a heated bowl large enough to toss the pasta in.

Heat the olive oil very hot in a small saucepan. Pour it over the mixture in the bowl about two minutes before the pasta is cooked. When the pasta is cooked and drained, toss it in the bowl and serve with toasted bread crumbs to sprinkle on top.

&

PASTA CU FINUCCHI
(Pasta With Fennel)

Wild fennel grows all over the hillsides in Sicily I am fortunate enough to live in Southern California, where the same is true. One can use the leaves of the anise bulb which is sold in supermarkets, but if it is at all possible to find the wild variety, it has a far superior taste.

FOR FOUR SERVINGS

½ cup fennel leaves, chopped fine	½ cup extra virgin olive oil
2 stalks, left whole	1 pound perciatelli pasta
½ cup Italian parsley leaves, chopped fine	sea salt
	black pepper
1 sprig mint, chopped fine	crushed red pepper
4 cloves garlic, chopped fine	toasted bread crumbs

Put up a large pot of salted water with a little olive oil and the whole fennel stalks in which to cook the pasta.

Meanwhile, chop the parsley, fennel, mint, and garlic. About three minutes before the pasta is cooked, place them in a heated serving bowl with salt, red and black pepper to taste. Pour over the olive oil, heated to nearly smoking.

When the pasta is cooked and drained, toss it with the ingredients in the bowl. Serve with more crushed red pepper if desired, and sprinkle with toasted bread crumbs.

⚜

PASTA 'A CARRITTERA
(Carter's-Style Pasta)

Tradition names this pesto sauce after the carters, who drove small horse carts carrying lemons, oranges, eggplants, and all the bounty of the island. For this meal, they would bring with them garlic and macaroni. Everything else they could always find along the way. The macaroni was cooked in a pot over an open fire, the pesto mortared in a bowl and warmed by the sun. Perhaps we cannot duplicate this idyllic scene, dining in the open air surrounded by lush terraced gardens and mountains beyond, but we certainly can enjoy the frank simple flavor of this dish.

Pesto is a sauce which is achieved by pounding together several ingredients to amalgamate their oils and flavors. The same results cannot be achieved by using a food processor or blender. To make a real pesto takes no longer than the time it takes to boil the pasta water and cook the pasta. If you are dissatisfied with your present mortar and pestle, there is an apparatus used in Japanese cuisine for grinding sesame seeds called a *sarebachi*. It consists of a ceramic bowl, glazed on both sides, with a rough interior surface, and a wooden pestle. I find it works better than any other mortar and pestle I have used. They are available in stores selling Japanese or health food cooking supplies.

FOR FOUR SERVINGS

1 pound penne or ziti tagliate	sea salt
5-7 cloves garlic, peeled	black pepper
1 bunch basil	crushed red pepper
½ cup extra virgin olive oil	grated locatelli or pecorino cheese
6 small Roma or Italian plum	
tomatoes, very red and ripe	

Put up a large pot of salted water with a little olive oil in which to cook the pasta. Place the garlic, a pinch of red pepper, a quarter teaspoon of salt, and enough olive oil to lubricate the process into the mortar. Using the pestle, reduce the garlic to a fine paste. Add the basil leaves, grinding them well into the paste, adding more olive oil as needed.

Unless you are using home-grown tomatoes with very thin skins, the tomatoes must be blanched to facilitate removal of their skins. Drop them in boiling water for one minute. Holding them, one at a time, in the air on a fork, peel away the skin with a paring knife. As each one is peeled, drop it into the pesto and squash it into the sauce. Add the remaining olive oil, mixing it together well. Check the salt. Keep the bowl on the stove, near the pasta pot to warm.

When the pasta is cooked and drained, toss it with the pesto in a heated bowl. Serve with plenty of grated cheese.

⚜

PASTA CA CUCUZZA
(Pasta With Sicilian Squash)

Cucuzza is a Sicilian squash of truly priapic proportions. They grow to be two to three feet long, with a crook at the end. Cucuzza is available only in summer and early autumn, making it a truly special treat. It is usually served with a wonderful pressed sheep's milk ricotta, coarsely grated on top. It goes under a variety of names, including ricotta salada, hard ricotta, grating ricotta, and a Greek version called mizithra.

FOR FOUR SERVINGS

1½ pounds cucuzza	1 28-ounce can Italian plum tomatoes,
1 pound ziti tagliate, cannorini,	without liquid, chopped, or 12 fresh,
or penne regate pasta	very ripe Italian plum tomatoes,
1 large onion, sliced	peeled and chopped
½ cup extra virgin olive oil	grated hard ricotta

Put up a large pot of water, with salt and olive oil, in which to cook the pasta.

Peel the cucuzza, cut it lengthwise, then slice it across in ½-inch pieces. In another six-quart pot, place the olive oil and onion. When the onion becomes clear, add the cucuzza and stir it well to distribute the olive oil. Add salt, pepper, a pinch of red pepper, and the tomatoes. Stir, cover, turn the heat to low, and simmer for 45 minutes, or until the cucuzza is soft. Do not cook the pasta until the cucuzza is ready. If you find the cucuzza has too much liquid, turn up the heat and leave the cover askew while the pasta cooks. When the pasta is cooked and drained, toss it with the cucuzza in the pot and serve with the grated hard ricotta.

PASTA MARINARA
(Sailor's-Style Pasta)

FOR FOUR SERVINGS

1 pound linguini fini

1 28-ounce can Italian peeled
   whole plum tomatoes

¹/₃ cup extra virgin olive oil

3-5 cloves garlic, chopped

2 teaspoons sugar

¹/₂ teaspoon dried oregano

sea salt

black pepper

crushed red pepper

grated pecorino or locatelli cheese

Put up the water with salt and a little olive oil in which to cook the pasta. While waiting for it to boil, prepare the sauce. Pour the contents of the can of tomatoes into a bowl. Squeeze the tomatoes with your hand to break them into small pieces. Place the garlic, a pinch of red pepper, and the olive oil in a skillet. Cook at medium heat for a minute or two. Do not allow the garlic to brown in any way. Turn off the heat to prevent splattering and add the tomatoes. Turn the heat back to low, add salt, black pepper, sugar, and oregano. Stir with a wooden spoon until a "creamy" consistency is reached. Cook for the remaining time at a low heat. The sauce should never boil.

When the pasta is cooked and drained, toss it with the sauce in a heated bowl. Serve with plenty of grated cheese.

CAVATEDDI CU BROCULI RABI
(Shell Pasta With Italian Broccoli)

Broculi rabi, a field green popular all over Sicily, is also called *rapini,* or Italian broccoli. The stems are covered with leaves and broccoli-like flowers. When little yellow flowers appear on these, the flavor is more bitter. Bunches with the thinnest stems are best, as they become fibrous and tough when thick.

FOR FOUR SERVINGS

1 ¼ pounds broccoli rabi
⅓ cup finely chopped onion
½ cup extra virgin olive oil
2 ripe Roma or Italian plum
    tomatoes, chopped
1 tablespoon pine nuts

1 pound cavatelli, or medium
    shell pasta
sea salt
black pepper
grated pecorino or locatelli cheese

Put up the water with salt and a little olive oil in which to cook the pasta. Chop the onion and tomato. Cut away the thick ends of the broccoli rabi, wash the remaining part thoroughly, and coarsely chop it.

Just after the water boils and the pasta begins to cook, put the olive oil and an onion in a skillet. Cook at medium heat until the onion begins to turn clear. Add the green vegetable, half at a time, and coat well with the oil and onion. Add salt, black pepper, the tomatoes, and pine nuts. Keep it all moving to keep it from burning. When the pasta is cooked and drained, toss it with the greens in a heated bowl. Serve with a little grated cheese to sprinkle on top.

PASTA CA MUDDICA E L'OVA

(Pasta With Bread Crumbs and Eggs)

Midweek in Lent, cold, damp, rainy. The kitchen quickly fills with the hearty aroma of this simple peasant meal.

FOR FOUR SERVINGS

4 hard-boiled eggs,
   peeled and whole

¼ cup extra virgin olive oil

3 cloves garlic, peeled, whole

¼ cup tomato paste

¾ cup water

2 sprigs Italian parsley, chopped

1 tin anchovies in olive oil

1 pound spaghetti

¾ cup toasted bread crumbs

black pepper

extra virgin olive oil

Put up a large pot of water with salt and a little olive oil in which to cook the pasta.

In a saucepan, place the olive oil together with the garlic. Heat gently, until the garlic begins to color, then discard it. Roll the hard-boiled eggs around in the oil until they are a light golden color, then remove them and save. Add the tomato paste and the water to the oil and stir until it achieves a creamy consistency. Add the eggs and continue cooking at very low heat for 10 minutes. Do not allow the sauce to boil. As this 10 minutes of simmering begins, start to cook the spaghetti in the boiling water.

Meanwhile, melt the contents of the anchovy tin in a covered double boiler. The anchovies must be melted in this manner because direct flame will cause them to become a salty bitter mess. If, like me, you do not own a double boiler, one can be arranged in your kitchen in a variety of ways. My favorite is a small, stainless steel bowl over a small saucepan. Put the water in the saucepan. The water in the saucepan should not touch the bowl, only its steam.

About two minutes before the pasta is cooked, whisk the anchovies with a fork and add them to the sauce. When the spaghetti is cooked and drained, place it in a heated bowl. Toss it with the sauce, some of the toasted bread crumbs, and the parsley. Place the eggs on top. Serve with more bread crumbs.

PASTA CU SPARACEDDU ARRIMINATU
(Pasta With Cauliflower)

In the Madonie Mountains in Sicily are cultivated the most extraordinary cauliflowers, called *sparaceddu*. They are deep green or streaked with purple and measure 14 inches across. Unlike our cauliflower, which is relatively mild in flavor, theirs is so strong-tasting that it must be blanched before any preparation.

In season they are bountiful and are canned for winter use, cooked into the sauce listed here.

FOR FOUR SERVINGS

1½ pounds cauliflower

1 pound gnochetti, cavatapi,
or medium shell pasta

⅓ cup extra virgin olive oil

2 cloves garlic, chopped fine

1 heaping tablespoon tomato paste
dissolved in ½ cup water

1 tin anchovies melted into
a paste in a double boiler

1 pinch saffron dissolved
in ⅓ cup water

sea salt

black pepper

crushed red pepper

4 sprigs Italian parsley, chopped

toasted bread crumbs
to sprinkle on top

Put up a large pot of water with salt and a little olive oil in which to cook the pasta.

Cut the cauliflower in half, and cut the florets away from the tough core. Then, coarsely chop the florets. Place the oil in a 9-inch skillet and turn the heat to medium. When the oil is hot, add the cauliflower and let it sauté for five minutes. Do not let the cauliflower take any color. Add the garlic, salt, pepper, and red pepper to taste. Next, add the tomato paste dissolved in water. Stir it all well, turn the heat down very low, cover, and cook about 20 minutes, or until the cauliflower is soft enough to chop into very small pieces with a wooden spoon. Stir it all very well. Add the anchovies and saffron, and cook for about two minutes, stirring so that it turns into a chunky paste. The word *arriminatu* means turned around or stirred up.

Toss the cauliflower with the cooked drained pasta in a heated bowl. Sprinkle the parsley on top. Serve with more red pepper and toasted bread crumbs sprinkled on top.

PASTA CHI SARDI A MARI
(Pasta With Sardines, Still in the Sea)

For those who are too poor to afford sardines, or for those in the mountains where fresh fish is difficult to come by, there is a version of pasta and sardines in which the sardines are still in the sea.

FOR FOUR SERVINGS

⅓ cup currants, plumped
   in white wine
1 medium onion, chopped fine
1½ cups fennel leaves, chopped fine
½ cup extra virgin olive oil
½ cup pine nuts
1 tin anchovies, melted in
   a double boiler

2 pinches saffron, dissolved
   in ¼ cup water
1 pound perciatelli pasta
sea salt
black pepper
crushed red pepper
½ cup toasted bread crumbs

Put up a large pot of water with salt and a little olive oil in which to cook the pasta.

Meanwhile, sauté the onion with a pinch of red pepper in the olive oil until it turns clear. Do not allow it to brown. Add currants, pine nuts, and fennel. Cook together for five minutes. If necessary, turn off the heat and warm it up two minutes before the pasta is cooked, at which time the saffron and anchovies are added. Check the salt and pepper.

Toss with the pasta in a heated bowl and serve with toasted bread crumbs to sprinkle on top, and crushed red pepper to taste.

PASTA FRIUTA
(*Fried Pasta*)

Pasta fruita recalls another era, when pasta was expensive and precious. The cheese and butter in this peasant dish enhanced the richness of the pasta. Its preparation, however, is tricky and requires practice, producing one portion at a time. Because of this, it is not recommended for more than two or four people. Even so, it is well worth trying.

For each portion, cook about ¼ pound fedelini or vermicelli pasta in abundant salted water without any oil. When it is cooked, drain it thoroughly and divide it into portions in individual pasta bowls.

Melt 1 tablespoon butter in a small, well-cured frying pan at low heat. Sprinkle 2 tablespoons grated locatelli or pecorino cheese over the melted butter, and when the cheese has melted, slip in one portion of pasta. Sprinkle 2 tablespoons of cheese on top. Cook it gently, scraping it loose if it begins to stick, until the cheese and butter on the bottom are a rich golden brown. Turn it over into a bowl, and slip it back into the pan to cook the other side. The pasta friuta may be kept hot in a warmed oven until all the portions are ready for serving.

❧

CERVOLUZZA
(*Sausage*)

In the Madonie, pigs are not penned but herded. Consequently, their meat is without much fat. Just before the pigs are slaughtered in the autumn, the chestnut season arrives, and the diet of chestnuts makes their meat very sweet.

The sausages produced here are simply exquisite. They are slightly thicker than a breakfast sausage and prepared in coils held together with wooden skewers. They are cooked either over an open fire or in a frying pan with a little Marsala wine. Although it is difficult to achieve the sweet flavor of that pork in America—unless of course you raise your own pig—it is possible to approximate the sausage either at home or with the help of an accommodating sausage shop. I have found that such shops generally require a five-pound minimum for special orders. You will probably also have to supply the cheese and white wine.

goat or sheep intestine sausage
casings (these are the proper
diameter)

3¾ pounds pork trimmings
containing 12 percent fat
(7 ounces), coarsely ground

1¼ pounds lean veal trimmings,
coarsely ground

5 tablespoons ground black pepper

1½ cups dry white wine

3 heaping tablespoons very dry
caciocavalo or imported
provolone cheese, grated

1½ tablespoons sea salt

2 tablespoons fennel seeds

2 tablespoons unbleached flour

Mix the ingredients together very well and stuff into the casing. Do not twist off individual sausages, but rather, make them in coils to fit a large skillet, or about 7 inches in diameter if barbecuing. Hold these coils together with wooden skewers so that they will remain intact when turned over in cooking.

To cook sausage in a frying pan, slowly heat a well-cured iron skillet until it is very hot. Turn the heat to high, and brown the sausage thoroughly. When turning the sausage to brown the other side, turn off the heat to prevent a grease fire. When the sausage is browned on both sides, add ¼ cup Marsala, again turning off the heat. Cook at medium until the alcohol has evaporated, then turn down the heat to low, cover, and cook for 15 minutes. Lift the sausage out of the pan onto a serving dish.

٭

STINCU D'AGNEDDU STUFFATU
(Lamb Shank Stew)

This simple stew is great on a rainy day. Serve it with plenty of great bread and bundles of napkins.

FOR FOUR SERVINGS

4 lamb shanks

3 cloves garlic, whole and peeled

1 sprig rosemary

1 28-ounce can Italian
plum tomatoes •

1 pound green beans

2 carrots, cut in thirds

2 tablespoons extra virgin olive oil

1 cup dry white wine

sea salt

black pepper

Pass the contents of the can of tomatoes through a food mill fitted with the smallest screen to remove the seeds. Scrape into the bowl any pulp that has stuck to the bottom and sides of the mill.

Heat the olive oil in a large pot. Add the garlic and the lamb shanks. Brown the shanks on all sides. When the garlic begins to turn brown, however, discard it. Remove the lamb from the pot and pour off all the fat.

Return the lamb to the pot and when it is heated, add the white wine and sea salt. Cook for a couple of minutes until the alcohol has evaporated. Add the tomato, carrots, rosemary, and black pepper. Cook at a slow simmer, covered, for one hour.

Skim off all the fat which has collected around the top of the pot. Add the green beans and continue cooking, covered, at a simmer for an additional 45 minutes to one hour. Skim off the fat again, check the salt, and serve.

⚜

MULINCIANI A PALMIGIANA
(Eggplant Palmigiana)

Eggplant palmigiana has nothing to do with Parma or parmesan cheese. It is originally Sicilian. The palmigiana refers to the look of the layered eggplant in the pan, reminiscent of a palm-thatched roof.

FOR FOUR SERVINGS

2 eggplants, about 1¼ pounds each	2 tablespoons white raisins
unbleached flour for dusting	or sultanas
extra virgin olive oil for frying	3 tablespoons pine nuts
⅓ pound caciocavalo or	sea salt
mozzarella, cut into thin strips	

FOR THE TOMATO SAUCE

3 tablespoons extra virgin olive oil	1 sprig basil
2 cloves garlic, whole and peeled	2 teaspoons sugar
1 28-ounce can Italian	sea salt
plum tomatoes	black pepper
1 heaping tablespoon tomato	
paste, dissolved in ¼ cup water	

Peel the eggplants. Cut them lengthwise in slices ½-inch thick. If the slices are very long, cut them in half. Liberally salt each slice and stack them in a shallow bowl. Place a dish upside down on top and put a light weight, such as a full can of tomatoes, on top of that. Keep the eggplant in the press for at least two hours. This process will drain out the acid liquid which causes eggplant to taste bitter and act like a sponge when fried.

After the time has elapsed, wipe or rinse off the salt and pat the slices dry. Heat 2 inches of olive oil in a skillet over medium heat until hot. Dust each slice with flour before frying. Cook to a rich golden brown, and drain between brown paper until everything else is ready for assembly.

Now it is time to prepare the tomato sauce. Pass the tomatoes and half the liquid from the can through the smallest screen of a food mill to remove the seeds. Scrape into the bowl any pulp that has stuck to the bottom of the mill. Place three tablespoons of olive oil in a saucepan, together with the garlic. Sauté the garlic in the olive oil until it is a light golden color and discard it. Stir in the tomatoes, add the sugar, salt, tomato paste, basil, and black pepper. Cook at a simmer for 10 minutes.

"Grease" the bottom of a loaf pan, preferably made of terra cotta, with tomato sauce. Line it with a layer of eggplant. Place a layer of cheese on top, a sprinkle of the raisins and pine nuts, and a drizzle of tomato sauce. Continue this operation for about four layers. Bake in a 375° oven for half an hour. Serve hot or at room temperature.

'A CUCINA RICCA

(The Cuisine of the Rich)

SPROGGHIU PITITTU
(Antipasti)

Il pasto are the Italian words for "the meal." An antipasto refers to food taken outside of the meal before *il primo piatto*, or first course of the meal. The Sicilian term for antipasto is *sprogghiu pitittu*. Literally translated, it means to "undress the appetite," expressing the whole point of an appetizer, to tease and excite the taste buds and lay bare one's hunger.

Whenever possible, I suggest serving the antipasto at a location other than at the dining table. Your guests should then have their appetites in a proper state of deshabille when they are called to table.

CAPUNATINA
(Eggplant and Olive Salad)

My favorite recipe for *capunatina* is the one listed here, which reads like a history lesson in the foreign occupation of Sicily. The eggplant is native, first spied by Odysseus in his travels. The olives were brought by the ancient Greeks, who colonized Sicily for an olive grove. From the North Africans came the raisins and almonds, offset by vinegar and red pepper; the celery from the more temperate Norman climes. The New World via Spain contributed tomato and a most unlikely ingredient, unsweetened cocoa powder.

2 large eggplants, weighing about
2 1/2 pounds together
1 pound whole, large green olives
3 ribs celery
1/4 cup sultanas or white raisins
1/3 cup extra virgin olive oil
2 tablespoons red vinegar

1/4 cup slivered almonds
2-3 teaspoons unsweetened
cocoa powder
sea salt
black pepper
crushed red pepper

FOR THE TOMATO SAUCE

2-3 cloves garlic
3 tablespoons extra virgin olive oil
1 16-ounce can Italian plum
tomatoes
2 teaspoons sugar

1 sprig basil
sea salt
black pepper

Smash each olive on a wooden board with a meat pounder or kitchen mallet. This is done to facilitate the pitting and also to release the oils through the olives. If you use pitted olives, it simply doesn't taste the same. Place the olive pieces in a small bowl and, while preparing the eggplant, soak them in three changes of cold water to remove the excess salt.

Peel the eggplant. Cut in half lengthwise and then slice into ½-inch-thick slices. Cross-cut it in half-inch pieces so that the chunks are about ½-inch thick and 1½ inches long.

Cut the celery in thin slices across the length of the ribs.

Place the olive oil in the bottom of a pot and add the celery. Sauté for about 5 minutes. Do not allow it to brown. Add the eggplant. Coat it in the olive oil and cook for about 5 minutes. Keep it moving so it doesn't burn or stick. Drain the olives and add them to the pot, mixing them in well. Stir in the raisins. Add salt and black pepper. Cover and cook at low heat for about 40 minutes. Stir from time to time.

Meanwhile, prepare the tomato sauce. Place the olive oil and the whole peeled garlic cloves in a small saucepan. When the garlic begins to turn golden on all sides, discard it.

Pour the contents of the can of tomatoes into a bowl and break the tomatoes into small pieces by squeezing them with your hand. Stir the tomatoes into the olive oil and add the sugar, salt, black pepper, and basil. Cook at a simmer for 10 minutes.

When the eggplant is cooked, remove the lid and boil away any liquid that separates from the mixture when it is pushed aside with a wooden spoon. Add the tomato sauce and cook uncovered for 10 minutes.

Remove from heat and add the vinegar and crushed red pepper to taste. Turn the capunatina into a serving bowl. Stir in the cocoa powder and slivered almonds. Stir from time to time while it cools. When it is room temperature refrigerate, bringing it out of the refrigerator one hour before serving.

Serve it with good bread—scoop it up Moroccan style.

PIPI SUTT'OGGHIU
(Bell Pepper Salad)

For this salad, select bell peppers that do not have deep indentations. Wash and dry them. With a pepper on the end of a fork, hold it close to the fire of a stove burner until the skin turns black. Turn the pepper until the skin is singed on all sides. This is the traditional method, but perhaps an easier way is to put all the peppers being used in the broiler close to the flame, turning them to achieve the same result.

Whichever method is chosen, when the peppers are cool enough to handle, peel off the charred skin, remove the core and the seeds, and slice them in strips. Arrange the strips in a neat pattern on a serving dish and top each layer with some chopped garlic, salt, and a pinch of dried oregano, plus a drizzle of extra virgin olive oil.

INSALATA 'I CALAMARI
(Squid Salad)

FOR EIGHT SERVINGS

5 pounds squid

1 head garlic

3 lemons

2 teaspoons capers

extra virgin olive oil

sea salt

black pepper

Cleaning squid is a simple process. Alongside the sink place two bowls of cold water, a small cutting board, and a sharp knife. In addition, keep cold water from the tap running gently.

Separate the tentacles from the sac by pulling the tentacles away with a slight twist. Most of the entrails will come away with it. Cut off the tentacles just forward of the eyes. Discard from the eyes back. In the center of the ring of tentacles is a hard, round ball containing the beak and the entire digestive system. Push it through and discard it. If the tentacles are large, cut off the suction pads and divide the ring in two or three sections. Rinse them and place the tentacles in one of the bowls.

Working under the running water, squeeze the sac of the squid to remove the jelly. Be sure to remove the bone which looks like a strip of cellophane and is attached at the top of the sac.

Tear off the fins. Remove the skin, rubbing it under running water, and then peel it away. Remove the skin on the sac in the same way and place both parts in the other bowl.

When all of the squid are cleaned, change the water in both bowls. Cut the sacs in trapezoid shaped rings about 1½ inches at the widest. Place them in the same bowl as the tentacles. Cut the fins into triangles. Change the water in the bowl one or two more times until it is clear.

Put up a 4-quart pot with water to boil. Meanwhile, peel and chop the garlic very fine. Working over a bowl to collect the juice, peel, seed, and chop two of the lemons. Juice the third.

When the water is boiling, drain the squid and cook it in the boiling water for 15 to 30 seconds. As a general rule, squid is crunchy when undercooked, rubbery when overcooked. The difference here is obviously a matter of seconds.

Drain the cooked squid and combine immediately with the lemon, lemon juice, and garlic. Then salt, adding plenty of extra virgin olive oil, some black pepper, and the capers. This fine dish is best served at room temperature.

∾⚓∾

BACCALARU A GHIOTTA
(Dried Salted Codfish Salad)

The art of preserving codfish by drying and salting was taught to the Sicilians by the Normans. Scandinavians still eat this delicacy they call *stokfish*.

In Sicily *baccalaru* is always a part of a Christmas Eve feast, a meatless meal of fish and vegetables.

In this country in recent years, dried salted codfish, also called *baccalá*, has become difficult to find. If you are fortunate enough to locate it, however, this recipe will turn it into a delicacy not to be missed.

FOR EIGHT SERVINGS

2 pounds dried salted codfish

4 comice pears or other type
   buttery pears

4 crisp apples

½ pound white potatoes peeled,
   cut, and boiled as for
   potato salad

1-2 red onions halved and sliced

6 green Roma or Italian plum
   tomatoes cut into sixths

2 ribs celery sliced thin

½ cup green olives pitted
   in large pieces

½ cup black olives pitted
   in large pieces

¾ to 1 cup extra virgin olive oil

3 tablespoons red wine vinegar

sea salt

black pepper

Soak the codfish in plenty of cold water for 3 days. Change the water twice a day. It is not necessary to refrigerate it, but keep it covered in a cool place. The soaking will reconstitute the fish and wash away the salt. When the soaking is completed, remove the baccalaru, rinse it under cold water, and place it in a platter to drain.

Halve, core, and peel the fruit. Place it in a large pot of fresh water and bring it slowly to a boil. The addition of crisp apples and buttery pears to the cooking liquid is a very old custom. It gives the baccalaru a subtle sweetness that is most complementary.

Meanwhile, prepare the other ingredients. When the water comes to a boil slip in the codfish and cook for five minutes. Remove it from the pot and when it is cool enough to handle, shred it, removing the skin and bones. Toss it in with the onions, tomatoes, olives, and celery. Add the vinegar and toss. Add potatoes, salt, and olive oil. Carefully toss it all together and add black pepper. Serve slightly chilled.

SALAMI 'I TUNNU 'NSTEMPERATA
(Salami of Tuna in Stemperata)

In Sicilian cooking there are several sauces or toppings that create a subtle sweet and sour flavor. These are called *turnagustu*, which means "turning taste." Stemperata is one of these.

FOR SIX SERVINGS

1 12-ounce can chunk light tuna in spring water	½ cup green olives, chopped fine
¼ cup extra virgin olive oil	¼ cup sultanas or white raisins, chopped fine
2 eggs	2 tablespoons celery, chopped very fine
1½ tablespoons capers	extra virgin olive oil
coarse black pepper	flour for dusting
2 ribs celery	

Place the contents of the tuna can in a doubled cheesecloth and squeeze it to remove all the water. Turn it into a bowl and mash it until it is smooth. Mix in the eggs thoroughly and add black pepper and capers.

Put up a large pot of water with two ribs of celery. While waiting for it to boil, form the salami. Place a 15-inch square of double cheesecloth on a work surface. Flour it and put the tuna mixture on it close to one edge in the shape of a fat salami. Loosely roll it up in the cheesecloth and tie it at the ends. When the water boils, place it gently in the pot. Be sure the pot is wide enough to accommodate the length of the salami, as it will swell during cooking. Cook it at a simmer for about an hour.

Remove it from the pot and when it is cooled refrigerate it until it is cold. Peel off the cheesecloth and cut it with a serrated knife in ¼-inch slices. Arrange them on a serving platter and drizzle olive oil on top.

Chop and mix the olives, sultanas, and celery. Spoon it on top.

Remove dish from the refrigerator 45 minutes before serving.

❧

INSALATA 'I CACUOCCIULI
(Artichoke Salad)

FOR SIX SERVINGS

2½ pounds fresh "baby" artichokes as prepared for 'a Frittedda	1 heart of a bunch of celery
4 lemons	extra virgin olive oil
1 tin anchovies in olive oil	salt

After the artichokes are peeled and cut, place a pot of water on the stove with the juice of two lemons and their rinds. When the water boils, add the drained artichokes, cover, and cook at medium heat for 20 minutes or until tender. Drain and run briefly under cold water to stop the cooking process.

When the artichokes are cool enough to handle, arrange a layer on a serving platter with the cut side down and in a spade shape resembling that of an artichoke leaf. Salt and drizzle olive oil. Arrange the next layer atop the first. Salt and drizzle olive oil after each layer. Decorate the top with the anchovies.

In the center of this artichoke "leaf" stick the celery heart straight up. Serve at room temperature. If it must be prepared in advance, add the anchovies and celery just before serving.

I always wondered why my grandfather Papa Andrea decorated this dish with celery, until I saw an artichoke plant. The celery heart looks like an artichoke stalk in miniature.

CACUOCCIULI MANDORLATA
(Artichokes With Almond Sauce)

As part of an antipasto, half an artichoke is appropriate for each serving. This sauce is also an excellent dip for cold steamed asparagus.

6 artichokes	juice of ½ lemon
1½ cups almond meal	1 teaspoon red wine vinegar
2 tablespoons flour	1 tablespoon sugar
2 cups water	¼ cup + 1 tablespoon extra virgin
¼ cup onion, chopped	olive oil
extremely fine	2 tablespoons capers
2 anchovies, melted in a double	sea salt
boiler with a little of their oil	black pepper

LIQUID FOR STEAMING

juice and rind of 1 lemon
¼ cup white wine
water

Cut about an inch off the top of each artichoke. Cut off the points of the remaining leaves with scissors. Spread each artichoke with your hand and rinse the inside under cold running water. Shake the artichokes dry. Rub each one with lemon and place them upside down on the rack of a steamer. Trim the stems so that the lid of the pot just fits. Place the steaming liquid in the bottom portion of the steamer and cook the artichokes for about 35 minutes or until tender.

Meanwhile, prepare the sauce. Melt the anchovies in a double boiler. Remove them from the heat and whisk in the lemon juice, vinegar, sugar, and ¼ cup olive oil. In a separate bowl, dissolve the flour in the water.

In a saucepan, sauté the onion in a tablespoon of olive oil until golden brown. Add the almond meal and stir together for a couple of minutes. Salt. Slowly add the water and flour mixture and cook for 10 to 15 minutes, stirring constantly until the sauce is thick and smooth and the flour taste is cooked away. Remove it from the heat and while whipping the sauce add the anchovy mixture very slowly. Then add a small amount of black pepper. Let the sauce cool, stirring from time to time to allow the steam to escape.

When the artichokes are cooked and cool enough to handle, cut them in half. Remove the choke and pointy leaves from the center with a spoon. When the sauce is cooled, fill each of these cavities with the sauce and decorate the top with capers. Serve chilled.

⚜

BABALUCCI
(Snails)

Babalucci are land snails with brown and white shells and are about the size of a nickel. They are plentiful in Sicily and live among the patches of wild fennel. They are difficult to find in markets outside of the great Italian enclaves of the eastern United States. If, however, you choose to forage them, rigorous precautions must always be taken, since in this country people would rather poison snails than eat them.

If you do find them in a market, observe the following process before cooking. Place your store-bought babalucci in a tightly woven basket with good airflow. Rinse them in cold water and shake out all excess. Sprinkle yellow cornmeal over them until they are barely covered with it. Cover the basket with a damp dish-towel, and fasten the towel securely to the basket with a piece of string to prevent the babalucci from escaping.

After a day rinse the snails clean and add fresh cornmeal. Continue this process of rinsing and changing the cornmeal, allowing the snails to purge themselves of their impurities, for a total of three days.

If you have acquired your babalucci from a questionable source but you know for certain that they are the correct type of edible snail, continue purging them of their impurities in the above manner for a total of ten days.

After the purging is complete, place the babalucci in a large pot. Add enough cold water to cover them. Place a lid securely on top of the pot. Weight it to prevent them from escaping. Soak them for about four hours until they poke out of their shells.

Stir the babalucci with a wooden spoon handle. Discard any snails which float to the top, as these have not made it from the fennel patch to this moment and there is no way of knowing how long ago they met their demise.

The babalucci are now ready to be cooked and eaten. If all this preparation seems to be a rather arduous task, the delicate sweetness of these creatures is well worth the effort.

Papa Andrea always cooked babalucci in a picante tomato sauce sweetened with slices of onions.

6 pounds snails, prepared in
  the manner stated

$^1\!/_3$ cup extra virgin olive oil

2 medium onions, sliced

2 28-ounce cans Italian
  plum tomatoes

3 teaspoons sugar

2 pinches dried oregano

sea salt

black pepper

crushed red pepper

Pour contents of the cans of tomatoes in a bowl. Squeeze the tomatoes by hand to break them into small pieces.

Combine olive oil, onion, and red pepper in a pot large enough to later hold the snails. Sauté the onion until it is clear; then add the tomatoes, salt, sugar, and black pepper. Simmer for 15 minutes, stirring from time to time.

Turn up the heat and when the sauce begins to boil, add the drained snails. Cook for no more than five minutes. Remove from the heat immediately, as overcooking will make the snails tough and rubbery.

At each place set a pin or a toothpick for removing the snails from their shells. Serve with good bread.

ARANCINI
(Rice Balls)

Arancini means "little oranges." The name refers to their shape and to the interior color, made orange by the addition of saffron. Arancini are best served whole as an antipasto. However, they can also be served as a first course, split, with tomato sauce on top. This is Papa Andrea's recipe.

2 pounds arborio rice

2 cups locatelli or imported
  pecorino cheese, grated

1 cup caciocavalo or imported
  provolone, grated

6 eggs

2 pinches saffron, dissolved in
  $^1\!/_4$ cup water

2 teaspoons milk

flour for dusting

bread crumbs for dusting

sea salt

black pepper

olive oil for frying (about 2 quarts)

FOR THE TOMATO SAUCE

1 28-ounce can Italian plum tomatoes	1 tablespoon tomato paste dissolved in ¹/₃ cup water
¹/₂ small onion, chopped fine	2 teaspoons sugar
¹/₄ pound mushrooms, chopped fine	1 sprig basil
	¹/₂ cup peas
¹/₂ pound ground veal	sea salt
¹/₈ pound ground pork	black pepper

The night before, or six hours before preparation, cook the rice in abundant, lightly salted water until it is slightly underdone. Drain thoroughly and mix in the saffron dissolved in water evenly.

When the rice has cooled slightly, add four of the eggs and the cheese and black pepper. Place the mixture in a shallow bowl. Cover with a dish towel and set it in a cool place, not the refrigerator, to set up.

The next day, about an hour before beginning to form the arancini, prepare the tomato sauce. Pass the contents of the can of tomatoes through a food mill, using the disk with the smallest holes, to remove the seeds. Scrape into the bowl any pulp that has stuck to the bottom of the mill.

Coat the bottom of a 1¹/₂-quart saucepan with olive oil and add the onion. Set heat to medium and sauté the onion until clear. Do not allow it to take any color. Add the chopped mushrooms. Salt. Continue to sauté until the liquid given off by the mushrooms is mostly evaporated. Add the pork and veal, breaking it into small bits with a wooden spoon. Continue to sauté until it is cooked. Add the tomato paste and continue to cook for a minute or two until it thickens. Add the tomatoes, sugar, basil, nutmeg, and black pepper. Turn down heat to low and simmer for 40 minutes, stirring occasionally. Do not allow it to boil.

When the sauce has finished cooking, remove about 1 cup of the meat and mushrooms from the sauce, using a slotted spoon, and place it in a small bowl.

Cook the peas and place them in another bowl.

Cover a work surface with waxed paper. If you are right-handed, line your left palm with the rice mixture, place a scant tablespoon of the meat-and-mushroom mixture in the center with a few peas, and roll up the rice into a ball so that the meat is in the center. Add more rice if necessary so that the ball ends up being the size of a Valencia orange. Roll it in flour and place it on the waxed paper. Continue until all of the arancini are formed to this point. Beat the eggs with the milk and wash each arancini in it, returning them to the waxed paper. Now coat each one with bread crumbs.

Meanwhile, heat the oil in a 3½-quart pot to 350°, which is the temperature at which a small square of bread will brown quickly but not burn.

Lower the arancini a few at a time into the hot oil and fry them until they are a rich golden brown. Remove from the pot with a slotted spoon and roll them on brown paper to remove the excess oil. They may be kept warm uncovered in a 300° oven until ready to serve.

CAZZIDDI
(Potato Croquettes)

FOR SIXTEEN CROQUETTES

2 pounds red or white potatoes	black pepper
1 cup grated locatelli or imported pecorino cheese	flour for dusting
	bread crumbs for dusting
4 eggs	olive oil for deep frying
8 anchovies, chopped	(about 2 quarts)

Peel and cut the potatoes as for potato salad. Boil them in lightly salted water until cooked but quite firm. Drain the potatoes and begin to mash them. Add the anchovies while the potatoes are still very hot so that they will melt. Continue mashing and add two eggs, cheese, and black pepper. When the potato mixture is well cooled, begin to form the croquettes.

With floured hands, form a small handful of the potatoes into a cylinder 1½ inches thick and 3 inches long. Carefully roll it in flour, then the beaten egg, then bread crumbs, following the same method as for Arancini.

Heat the oil in a 3½ quart pot until it is 350°, which is the temperature at which a small square of bread will brown quickly but not burn. Gently slip in the croquettes a few at a time. When they are a rich color, remove them from the oil and drain on brown paper.

They may be kept warm in a 300° oven uncovered until they are ready to serve. Arrange them in a pyramid on a platter.

PIPI CHINI A NANA GIAMBALVO

(Nana Giambalvo's Stuffed Peppers)

The mother of my aunt, who married my mother's brother, was Nana Giambalvo. She came from Santa Margherita di Belice, a town in the Sicilian province of Agrigento. The inhabitants of Santa Margherita are known for their accomplishments in law, politics, and medicine. Nana Giambalvo's achievement was cooking: her stuffed peppers are the best I've ever eaten.

FOR EIGHT TO TEN SERVINGS

10-12 small bell or long, light green peppers. These peppers are sometimes called Italian or Hungarian peppers.

³/₄ pound chopped veal

¹/₄ pound chopped pork

¹/₂ medium onion, chopped fine

¹/₂ cup arborio rice

2 eggs, hard-boiled, peeled, and chopped

1-2 eggs, beaten (raw)

2 tablespoons pine nuts

sea salt

black pepper

extra virgin olive oil

4 scrapes nutmeg

FOR THE TOMATO SAUCE

2 tablespoons extra virgin olive oil

¹/₂ medium onion, chopped fine

1 28-ounce can Italian plum tomatoes

1 teaspoon sugar

1 sprig mint

sea salt

black pepper

Cook the rice in abundant boiling salted water. When it is slightly underdone, drain it and run it under cold water to stop the cooking process.

While the rice is cooking, prepare the tomato sauce. Pass the contents of the can of tomatoes through a food mill, fitted with the disk with the smallest holes, in order to remove the seeds. Scrape into the bowl any pulp that has stuck to the bottom of the mill.

Put the olive oil and the onion in a saucepan. Set heat to medium and when the onion turns clear add the tomatoes, salt, sugar, pepper, and mint. Cook at a simmer for 15 minutes, stirring from time to time. Do not allow it to boil.

While the tomato sauce is cooking, prepare the stuffing. Grease a skillet with about 1 tablespoon olive oil. Add the onion and sauté at medium heat until it turns clear, then add the chopped meats and turn the heat up. Mix it with the onion and break it into small pieces with a wooden spoon. Salt. When the meat is thoroughly cooked, add about half a cup of tomato sauce. Remove it from the heat and transfer it to a bowl. Mix in the rice. Allow it to cool thoroughly. Then add the chopped hard-boiled eggs, raw eggs, pine nuts, black pepper, and nutmeg. Check the salt.

Prepare the peppers for stuffing. Wash and dry them thoroughly. If using bell peppers, cut off the top in a straight cut as near to the top as possible. If using the long green peppers, cut open the stem end on the diagonal to prevent the stuffing from running out when they are lying down in the pan. In either case, remove the seeds and the "ribs" as best as possible. Rub each pepper with olive oil inside and out. Stuff the peppers loosely. Place about 1 tablespoon of tomato sauce on top and bake at 350° for 30 to 40 minutes. These peppers may be served hot or cold.

TORTA 'I CACUOCCIULI
(Artichoke Pie)

Torta 'i cacuocciuli was one of the delights of my childhood. The crust is made from a recipe I have from my great-grandfather Cologero Vilardi. As a child, I ate it as a main course. But I have served it as an antipasto cut in small slices, and it works well.

FOR ONE 9-INCH DIAMETER PIE (2 INCHES DEEP)

2 pounds "baby" artichokes prepared in the same manner as for 'a Frittedda	1 cup mozzarella, coarsely grated
	2 tablespoons bread crumbs
¼ cup extra virgin olive oil	6 eggs
½ cup grated locatelli or imported pecorino cheese	½ cup cream
	salt
½ cup caciocavalo or imported provolone cheese, grated	black pepper

FOR THE CRUST

2 cups unbleached flour, sifted	½ cup vegetable shortening
1 teaspoon salt	1 tablespoon water
2 eggs, beaten	1 tablespoon cognac

When the artichokes have been prepared, heat the olive oil in a non-reactive skillet. Add the drained artichokes, salt, and turn them in the oil for a couple of minutes. Turn down the heat, cover, and cook for 20 minutes or until they are cooked but firm. Stir from time to time to make sure they are not burning.

When they are cooked, remove the cover, turn up the heat, and sauté the artichokes until they are a light golden color. Remove them from the oil and set them aside to cool.

Now prepare the crust. Sift together the flour and salt. Cut in the shortening until it is the size of split peas. Cut in the eggs as well. Add the water and cognac. Form the dough into a ball, cover, and let it rest for 10 minutes.

This would be a good time to prepare the filling. Beat together the eggs, cream, grated caciocavalo, grated locatelli, and black pepper.

After the dough has rested, roll it out into a 12-inch-diameter circle about $3/16$TH an inch thick. Press it into a 9-inch-diameter, 2-inch-deep baking pan with a removable bottom. Sprinkle the bottom of the crust with the bread crumbs and then the mozzarella in an even layer. Arrange the artichoke hearts in a neat layer with the cut side down. Pour the egg mixture over all and bake in the center of a preheated 375° oven for an hour or until a rich golden brown.

Roll out the leftover dough and cut out decorative shapes with a cookie cutter. I prefer farm animals. Bake them separately and when the pie is baked, stand them up on top as decoration. Serve slightly warm from the oven.

I Primi Piatti

(First Courses)

$\mathcal{P}$apa Andrea had in his repertoire a vast assortment of first course dishes, ranging from simple pastas and soups of the cuisine of the poor to the more complex ones listed in this section.

On the subject of pasta, it has been noted that if the various cultures of Italy have produced nothing else in the past 2,500 years, they have produced an entire people, each of whom can cook a dish of pasta blindfolded, standing on their heads, asleep.

⚜

SUPPA 'I PISCI
(Fish Soup)

FOR FOUR SERVINGS

2 pounds fish, composed of three different kinds, such as swordfish, shark, sea bass, cod, orange roughy

2 medium-sized onions, thinly sliced

2 cloves garlic, chopped

4 stalks celery, thinly sliced

4 sprigs Italian parsley, chopped

2-3 bay leaves

½ cup extra virgin olive oil

22 peppercorns

1 28-ounce can Italian plum tomatoes, drained of their liquid, coarsely chopped

1 cup dry white wine

sea salt

black pepper

Cut the fish in pieces about 1¼ inches square. Leave them to soak in a bowl of cold salted water. This process will soften, sweeten, and remove excessively strong flavors from the fish.

Meanwhile, prepare the other ingredients. In an ovenproof casserole with a lid (earthenware is best), mix together all of the ingredients except the fish, white wine, and bay leaves. Be sure to add salt. Gently slip the bay leaves on the bottom of the pot so that they don't break. Arrange the fish on top, moisten with the white wine. Add just enough water to barely cover the fish.

Cover and bake in a preheated 375° oven for exactly 40 minutes and serve.

PUPETTEDDI 'NBRUDU
(Meatball Soup)

FOR SIX SERVINGS

2 quarts water

¼ cup extra virgin olive oil

2 ribs celery, sliced thin

¾ teaspoon coarse sea salt

½ pound chopped veal

2 slices Italian bread (about
   2ounces) without the crust,
   soaked in milk and squeezed out

½ clove garlic, chopped fine

1 egg

3 tablespoons locatelli or imported
   pecorino cheese, grated

¼ pound fidelini or vermicelli
   pasta broken in thirds

¼ cup chopped Italian parsley

¾ teaspoon course sea salt

black pepper

grated cheese to sprinkle on top

Put the water, celery, olive oil, and salt in a pot. Cover and bring to a boil. Meanwhile, prepare the meatballs.

Mix together well the chopped veal, garlic, bread, egg, grated cheese, black pepper, and 1 tablespoon of chopped parsley. The best way to accomplish this is by hand.

When the water boils, form the meat mixture into balls about the size of filberts or hazelnuts. As each one is formed, drop it into the pot. When they are all in the pot, turn down the heat to "low," put the cover on askew, and simmer for 40 minutes. Stir from time to time.

Now add the pasta. When it is cooked, check the soup for salt, add the remaining parsley, and serve with grated cheese sprinkled on top.

BRUDU 'I GADDINA
(Chicken Soup)

1 3½-pound free-range chicken,
   including the neck, gizzard,
   liver, heart, and feet

3 large carrots, cut in thirds

3 ribs celery and their leaves,
   cut in thirds

2 large onions, quartered

12 sprigs Italian parsley

1 small bell pepper

6 Roma or Italian plum tomatoes

5 quarts water

2 tablespoons coarse sea salt

coarse ground black pepper

Rinse the chicken and remove any large pieces of fat from around the crop and the cavity. Place it, together with the other ingredients, in a large stockpot. Although many people are repulsed by chicken feet, remember that they add a heartiness to the soup which cannot be achieved by any other means.

Place the pot on the stove and, with the cover askew and the heat at medium, bring the contents slowly to a boil. Remove the scum that forms on top.

Now turn down the heat and cook at a simmer for three hours, still with the cover askew and removing the scum.

At this time turn off the heat and fish out the chicken and its parts. Place them on a platter. Strain the stock through a large, fine wire sieve into another pot or bowl and allow it to cool. Meanwhile, place the vegetables recovered from the stock into a food mill and reduce them to a fine puree. It is easier to use the disk with the largest holes first and then proceed to the one with the smallest, rather than trying to use the smallest from the outset.

By this time the stock will have cooled enough to remove the fat. Skim it off using a fat-straining device. Mix the puree into the stock and heat it uncovered to a good serving temperature. Check the salt and pepper.

If you are serving it as a soup, shred the meat of the chicken and add it. Serve with a small amount of grated locatelli or pecorino cheese. If you are using part of it for the risotto which follows, do not add the chicken.

❧

RISUTTU CHI FUNCI
(*Risotto With Mushrooms*)

When I was a boy, one cold day in February, so nasty a day that school was closed, my grandfather Papa Andrea looked out the window and, as if it were written on the steel gray Brooklyn sky, announced in Sicilian, "Today I will make risotto."

One of my aunts who was in the kitchen expressed her desire to watch because her risotto never tasted like his did. My grandmother, who was also there, warned her daughter not to take her eyes off her father, saying, "He's never shared this recipe with anyone and he's not going to share it with you!" Papa Andrea chuckled at such foolishness.

In order to make the risotto, a good chicken soup had to be made first. To make the chicken soup, a chicken had to be procured. My grandfather and I suited up for the elements and went on the four-block walk to the chicken market. We sang Sicilian songs on the way to warm us and to make the time go faster.

Inside the market, amidst the clucking and the horrendous odor of live poultry, we were greeted by the chickenmonger, who pointed my grandfather in the direction of his best chicken. "Do you take me for a fool?" Papa Andrea said. "That chicken isn't plump. It merely has her feathers puffed. I want that chicken over there." "With all respect, Maestro," voiced the chickenmonger, "anyone can see that the chicken you choose is a ball of fat!" Papa Andrea rejoined, "Better fat than feathers!"

And so the conversation went, each of them supporting their choice with the memories of other chickens which they each had championed or cursed in the past. Chickens long eaten, but not forgotten. After about twenty minutes of this perhaps playful exchange (one could never be sure), a decision was reached. The condemned chicken was weighed and paid for and sent to the back of the store to be slaughtered. My grandfather took me by the hand to witness this act. I believe he did this to teach me to show respect for food, that it doesn't merely appear in the supermarket on styrofoam trays wrapped in clear plastic.

On the way home, I carried the chicken. It was warm from the water used to clean it. My grandfather told me it would help keep me warm. After a few choruses of our songs, we were home again.

Papa Andrea rolled up his sleeves so that his long underwear showed, washed his hands, and tucked a dish towel in the waistband of his high pants as an apron. He rinsed the chicken, and as it drained he prepared the vegetables for the soup, my aunt hanging on every movement her father made, remembering her mother's words of warning. While the soup cooked, we ate lunch. It was chicken liver with marsala and onions. The livers were an offering from the chickenmonger as a sign of good faith.

When the soup was cooked, Papa Andrea strained the vegetables and added them to the broth, my aunt, of course, at his elbow. As dinnertime approached, he began to make the risotto, instructing my aunt on the careful addition of soup to the rice, adding more only when it had been absorbed, and stirring constantly. He added the sautéed mushrooms and later the peas. When it was cooked, he turned off the heat and with a flourish stirred in a handful of grated cheese, placed the lid on the pot, and with a sliding clap of his hands announced, "And now the risotto is finished."

By this time everyone else had come home from work and was bustling about, preparing for dinner. At one point he and I were alone in the kitchen. He quickly beat two eggs and stirred them into the risotto. Raising his fingers to his lips, he enlisted my silence on the matter.

From time to time over the years, my aunt would say how she made "u risuttu" and it just didn't taste like Papa's. She still doesn't know.

FOR SIX SERVINGS

8 cups chicken soup from the previous recipe

½ pound white or crimini mushrooms

2 tablespoons butter

3 tablespoons extra virgin olive oil

1 medium-sized onion, sliced thin

1 pound (about 2 cups) arborio rice

½ cup dry white wine

½ cup shelled peas

1 cup grated locatelli or pecorino cheese

2 eggs, beaten

sea salt

black pepper

Clean the mushrooms under running water with a mushroom brush. Do not soak them. Pat them dry and cut away the hard end of each stem. Cut each mushroom in quarters or sixths, depending on their size.

Pour two tablespoons of the oil into a skillet. Heat it at high heat until it is almost smoking. Add the mushrooms and salt. Sauté for 5 minutes. Remove from the heat and reserve for later use.

Heat the chicken soup in a covered pot, slowly, until it is at a trembling boil. Meanwhile, keeping them all in separate bowls, slice the onion; beat the eggs; and measure out the peas, white wine, and rice.

Place the butter and remaining olive oil in a heavy, 3½-quart pot. Set the heat to medium and when the butter has melted, add the onion. Sauté until clear. Do not allow it to brown in any way.

Now add the rice. Turn it in the pot until it is well coated and hot. If the rice scorches or sticks, the risotto will be ruined as the rice will not absorb the liquid.

Pour in the white wine and stir gently but constantly until it is completely absorbed by the rice. Add about ½ cup of the soup and continue to stir until it has been absorbed. Repeat this process, always stirring constantly. As the rice cooks, add the soup in smaller and smaller quantities so that as the cooking nears completion the soup is added a tablespoonful at a time. Adding the liquid in too large quantities will cause the risotto to be gummy and porridgelike. Adding too little at a time may cause it to burn. The proper consistency is creamy, but with each grain individuated and cooked all the way through. If the rice appears cooked but has a dry center, continue to add small quantities of soup and stir until this is remedied.

The cooking time from the first addition of the liquid is exactly 18 minutes. If the time varies, it is a good key to find the proper heat adjustment and/or liquid addition for your equipment and technique.

It is not necessary to use all the soup. If you find you need more, continue with boiling water.

After about 7 minutes of cooking time, salt. Add the sautéed mushrooms at about 14 minutes and the peas 2 minutes later.

When the risotto is cooked, remove from the heat and gently stir in ½ cup of the grated cheese and the beaten eggs. Cover and let it rest for three minutes before serving. Serve with additional grated cheese and black pepper.

❧

RISUTTU CHI CALAMARI
(Risotto With Squid)

FOR SIX SERVINGS

1 pound (about 2 cups) arborio rice	2¼ pounds medium-sized squid
½ medium-sized onion, chopped fine	¼ cup Italian parsley, chopped
	zest of half a lemon
¼ cup extra virgin olive oil	sea salt
1 cup dry white wine	black pepper

FOR THE STOCK

squid ink	1 medium-sized onion, quartered
6 cups water	1 tablespoon coarse sea salt
1 rib celery	

Clean the squid as for Insalata 'i Calamari, but reserve the ink sac. This sac is located between the eyes. Incise it and gently squeeze the ink into a small bowl.

Place the water, ink, onion, celery, and salt in a saucepan. Bring it slowly to a gentle boil and immediately turn it down to simmer.

Place the chopped onion and the olive oil in a heavy 3½ quart saucepan. Sauté it at medium heat until the onion turns clear. Do not brown it. Turn in the rice, and when it is well coated and warmed add half the white wine. Stir constantly and when it is well absorbed add the other half. Continue stirring and adding the stock as previously described until the rice is about three minutes from being cooked.

Now stir in the squid. When the rice is cooked, add two additionaltablespoons of stock, the parsley, and the lemon zest. Serve immediately with black pepper.

⚜

PASTA FRISCA
(Homemade Pasta)

Pasta found its way to Italy not through Marco Polo via China, as is often believed, but through Sicily via North Africa and Persia. In fact, there exist records of a macaroni factory from a Sicilian town named Trabia that predate Marco Polo's adventures by several hundred years.

For use with certain sauces, the delicacy of fresh, homemade pasta is incomparable. The process for making it, even without special equipment, is simple and not very time-consuming. In fact, the less processed the pasta is, the better it tastes. Even though one-step electric machines are very convenient, they tend to mix the dough too smooth and soft. It is always better to mix and knead the dough by hand and use a machine only for rolling and cutting. The hand-cranked machines allow for a greater variance of dough consistency. These machines are easily found at popular prices. If a machine is not being used, be sure that your rolling pin is a heavy one.

INGREDIENTS FOR HOMEMADE PASTA

Pasta flour is made from hard durum wheat or semolina. It is milled to a slightly finer consistency than yellow cornmeal, or polenta. If it is milled like traditional flour, the pasta will be gummy and too soft. Other basic ingredients in pasta are eggs, olive oil, salt, and water. Following is a list of ingredients proportioned for various amounts:

FOR 2 TO 3 SERVINGS

1¼ cups semolina	½ teaspoon salt
2 eggs	2 tablespoons water
2 teaspoons extra virgin olive oil	

FOR 6 TO 7 SERVINGS

3¾ cups semolina	1 teaspoon salt
5 eggs	¼ cup water
1 tablespoon extra virgin olive oil	

FOR 8 TO 10 SERVINGS

5 cups semolina	1½ teaspoons salt
8 eggs	⅓ cup water
1½ tablespoons extra virgin olive oil	

MIXING THE DOUGH

The way pasta dough is mixed forms a connection with a centuries-old tradition. Mound the semolina on a large wooden or marble work surface. Make a crater in the center of the mound. Break the eggs in the crater and add the olive oil and salt. Beat this mixture with a fork. When it is well beaten, use the fork to slowly draw in the semolina and mix it into the liquid. When this method proves to be unmanageable with a fork, use a metal dough scraper to thoroughly cut in all of the semolina. Add just enough water to form it into a heavy dough. Depending on weather conditions, you may need more water than is prescribed or, perhaps, none at all.

KNEADING THE DOUGH

Flour the work surface with semolina. Knead the dough by holding it in place with the palm of one hand and stretching it away from itself with the other. Fold it together and repeat this maneuver until the dough is elastic and shows a "pebbly" surface when the ball is broken in half. Cover the dough and let it rest for 10 minutes.

ROLLING THE DOUGH

If you are working with a hand-cranked pasta machine, cut off a piece of dough about the size of an orange. Flatten it with a heavy rolling pin. Flour it with semolina. Run it through the rollers of the machine set on the widest opening. Fold it in thirds and run it through again, keeping the widest opening. Repeat two or three more times until the dough achieves an elastic consistency and the texture of damp leather. Now roll it through set on the next opening. Fold the dough in half and roll it through that opening again. Continue this procedure until the second to the smallest opening of the rollers is reached. As the dough gets thinner, guide it with the back of your hand to prevent stretching or tearing. Now flour it well with semolina and fold it in half. Flour and fold again. Keep flouring and folding until it resembles a folded bedsheet. In fact, the pasta dough in this form is called *linsuola*, which is Italian for "bedsheet." Leave it on a well-floured portion of the board uncovered. Roll the rest of the dough and fold it into linsuola.

If you are not using a machine, roll out the dough using a heavy pin until it is about ¼-inch thick. Fold it in half and roll again. Continue folding and rolling until it is the consistency of damp leather. Now roll it into a large rectangle just thin enough to barely see the work surface through it. Flour it very well with semolina on both sides and fold it in the manner previously described.

CUTTING THE PASTA

Let the linsuola dry for 10 to 20 minutes until dry on the outer surface, but by no means crumbly.

If a machine is being used, unfold the linsuola and run them through the appropriate cutters of the machine. *Tagghiarini* is the Sicilian name for *tagliatelle* or *fettuccine*. Flour the tagghiarini well and leave them in loose coils on a board covered with a dish towel until ready for use.

If you are not using a machine, cut the linsuola with a sharp knife in ½ inch wide strips. Unfold the pasta and collect them in coils as previously described.

COOKING THE PASTA

Fresh pasta cooks very fast—in three minutes or less. Bring a large pot of water with salt and olive oil to a boil. Carefully drop in the coils of pasta. Stir with a large fork to make sure the pasta doesn't stick together. When it rises to the top, it is cooked.

TAGGHIARINI CA SARSA FRISCA
(Tagliatelle With Fresh Tomato Sauce)

When I was a boy, there was always great excitement when the Italian plum tomatoes appeared in the market during harvest time. Papa Andrea would make the *tagghiarini* by hand and sauce it in this delicate tomato sauce flavored with fresh basil and dusted with coarse-grated, hard, sheep's-milk ricotta.

These plum tomatoes make an appearance but once a year, and the incomparable flavor is still well worth waiting for.

FOR SIX SERVINGS

6 servings fresh tagghiarini	3-4 sprigs fresh basil
4 pounds Italian plum tomatoes,	sea salt
very ripe	black pepper
⅓ cup extra virgin olive oil	coarse-grated, sheep's milk,
2 cloves garlic, whole and peeled	hard ricotta (ricotta salata)

Blanch the tomatoes in boiling water for two minutes. Drain. While holding a tomato on the end of a fork, peel away the skin. Place all the tomatoes in a food mill fitted with the disk with the smallest holes and mill them to remove the seeds. Scrape into the bowl any pulp stuck to the bottom of the mill.

Pour the olive oil into a saucepan, add the garlic, and sauté gently until it is a pale golden color. Discard the garlic. Add the tomatoes and stir until the mixture is creamy. Salt and add the basil and black pepper. Cook for 40 minutes at a slow simmer. Be sure it does not boil.

Meanwhile, put up a large pot of water with salt and olive oil in which to cook the pasta. When the sauce is ready and the water has come to a boil, cook the pasta and drain it thoroughly. Serve a small amount of sauce over each portion of the tagghiarini. Sprinkle coarse-grated, hard ricotta on top.

⚜

TAGGHIARINI CHI CACUOCCIULI
(Tagliatelle With Artichokes)

FOR SIX SERVINGS

6 servings fresh tagghiarini	2 tablespoons tomato paste
16 baby artichokes	dissolved in ½ cup water
2 lemons	1 tablespoon sugar
⅓ cup extra virgin olive oil	2 sprigs fresh mint
3 cloves garlic, whole and peeled	sea salt
2 28-ounce cans Italian	black pepper
plum tomatoes	grated locatelli or pecorino cheese

Clean the artichokes as for Insalata 'i Cacuocciuli. Pass the tomatoes through a food mill fitted with the disk with the smallest holes to remove the seeds. Scrape into the bowl any pulp that has stuck to the bottom of the mill.

Place the olive oil and garlic in a saucepan. Sauté the garlic until it is pale golden and discard it. Drain the artichokes and add them to the saucepan. Sauté for five minutes. Keep them moving so they do not brown or burn. Add the tomato paste and continue to cook for a couple of minutes. Add the tomatoes, salt, black pepper, sugar, and mint. Cook uncovered at a gentle simmer for about 40 minutes until the artichokes are tender but firm.

Meanwhile, put up a large pot of water with salt and olive oil in which to cook the pasta. When the water boils and the artichokes are cooked, cook the pasta.

Drain thoroughly, turn it into a large warmed bowl, and toss it with some of the sauce. Divide it into portions in individual pasta bowls. Using a slotted spoon, distribute the artichokes equally among each portion. Place more sauce on top and serve with grated cheese.

❧

PASTA ALLA NORMA
(*Fresh Pasta With Eggplant*)

This dish of fresh pasta with eggplant, tomato sauce, and cheese was a favorite of the great Sicilian composer Vincenzo Bellini. It has been renamed after his most famous opera, *La Norma*.

FOR FOUR SERVINGS

4 servings fresh tagghiarini

1 or 2 eggplants, weighing a total of 1½ pounds

sea salt

extra virgin olive oil for frying

flour for dusting the eggplant

FOR THE TOMATO SAUCE

1 28-ounce can Italian plum tomatoes

2 cloves garlic, peeled and whole

¼ cup extra virgin olive oil

1 tablespoon tomato paste dissolved in ⅓ cup water

2 teaspoons sugar

2 sprigs fresh basil, chopped

sea salt

black pepper

⅓ to ½ pound ricotta salata (hard, sheep's milk ricotta), coarsely grated

Prepare the eggplant as for Mulinciani a Palmigiana. As it nears the end of its pressing time, put up a large pot of water with salt and a little olive oil in which to cook the pasta and begin to prepare the tomato sauce.

Pass the contents of the can of tomatoes through a food mill fitted with the disk with the smallest holes in order to remove the seeds. Scrape into the bowl any pulp that has stuck to the bottom of the mill.

Place the olive oil and the garlic in a saucepan and sauté at low heat until the garlic turns a light golden color. Discard it. Add the tomatoes, then the paste, sugar, salt, pepper, and basil. Stir well. Cook at low heat for 20 minutes. Do not allow it to boil.

Meanwhile, continue to prepare and fry the eggplant. Keep it hot uncovered in a 300° oven.

When all of the eggplant is done, cook the pasta in the boiling water. Drain it and toss it in a warmed serving bowl with some of the sauce and half of the cheese. Arrange the eggplant on top. Drizzle tomato sauce and sprinkle with cheese.

Serve immediately with a little more sauce and a sprinkling of cheese.

❦

MALFATTI MARINARA
("Badly Made" Pasta Marinara)

Malfatti means "badly made." In this case, it means pasta that is cut into irregular shapes.

FOR FOUR SERVINGS

4 servings fresh homemade
   pasta dough
1 recipe sauce from
   Pasta Marinara

½ cup locatelli or imported
   pecorino cheese, grated

Put up a large pot of water with salt and olive oil in which to cook the pasta. Meanwhile, prepare the pasta dough but do not cut it. Instead, unfold the linsuola or sheets and cut them with a fluted wheel cutter into irregular shapes measuring about two inches square. Flour them well with semolina and leave them scattered on the work surface covered with a dish towel.

Prepare the marinara sauce. When it is ready, cook the pasta in the boiling water. These malfatti may take longer to cook than other fresh pasta because of their size.

When they are cooked, drain them thoroughly and turn into a warmed oval serving platter. Toss gently with the marinara sauce. Serve immediately with grated cheese.

PERCIATEDDI CHI PISCI SPATA
(Perciatelli With Swordfish)

FOR FOUR SERVINGS

2 cloves garlic, whole and peeled

1 pinch crushed red pepper

⅓ cup extra virgin olive oil

8 Italian plum tomatoes, canned

¾ pound swordfish

1 cup fresh mint leaves, chopped

½ cup water

1 pound perciatelli pasta

¼ pound mozzarella,
    in small dice

sea salt

black pepper

extra virgin olive oil

Put up a large pot of abundant salted water with a little olive oil in which to cook the pasta.

Skin, bone, and cut the swordfish in small dice.

Place the tomatoes in a bowl and, using your hand, squeeze them into small pieces.

Chop the mint, peel the garlic, chop the mozzarella in small dice, and keep near the stove to warm but not melt.

Place the garlic, olive oil, and crushed red pepper in a skillet. Heat. When the garlic is golden on all sides, discard it. Stir in the tomatoes, salt, and 2 tablespoons of the mint. Simmer for five minutes.

Add the swordfish, black pepper, and water. Cook at a simmer for 15 to 20 minutes.

When the water boils, cook the perciatelli. Heat a large serving bowl with hot tap water and dry it. When the pasta is cooked and drained, toss it in the bowl with the sauce, mozzarella, and mint. Work quickly so it stays hot enough to melt the cheese. Serve immediately.

If swordfish is not available, thrasher shark is a good substitute.

❧

MACCARUNI 'A FURNU
(Baked Macaroni)

In *maccaruni 'a furnu* macaroni is baked with little meatballs, hard-boiled eggs, caciocavalo, and pecorino cheeses. It is flavored with tomato and salami. A very hearty dish, with big flavors, it is best served, in small quantities, as a first course.

FOR SIX SERVINGS

1 pound sedani, a smaller version
of rigatoni or
1 pound rigatoni pasta

3 tablespoons extra virgin olive oil

1/2 pound ground veal

2 sprigs Italian parsley, chopped

4 eggs

2 slices Italian bread, about
2 ounces, without the crust,
soaked in milk and squeezed out

1 cup locatelli or pecorino cheese,
grated

1/4 pound caciocavalo or imported
provolone cheese, cut in thin strips

2 slices soppresatta salami,
about 1/8 inch thick, cut in small dice

3/4 cup white wine

1 tablespoon tomato paste

2 cloves garlic, whole and peeled

1 28-ounce can Italian plum tomatoes

2 teaspoons sugar

2 tablespoons toasted bread crumbs

sea salt

black pepper

Put up a large pot of water with salt and olive oil to boil, in which to cook the macaroni.

Pass the contents of the can of tomatoes through a food mill fitted with the disk with the smallest holes in order to remove the seeds. Scrape into the bowl any pulp that has stuck to the bottom of the mill.

In a separate bowl, dissolve the tomato paste in the white wine.

Now begin to prepare the meatballs and the tomato sauce. Place the ground veal in a bowl, add the bread, parsley, one egg, 1/3 cup grated cheese, and black pepper. Mix these ingredients thoroughly by hand.

Place a sheet of waxed paper over a work surface. Form the mixture into balls about the size of a filbert or hazelnut and place them gently and neatly on the waxed paper.

When this is completed, put the garlic and olive oil in a heavy 9-inch skillet and turn on the heat to low. When the garlic begins to take color, discard it. Turn up the heat to medium and gently add the meatballs. Brown them on all sides. Turn off the heat to avoid splattering and add the white wine and tomato paste. Turn the heat back on and cook for several minutes until the alcohol has evaporated, gently turning the meatballs in the wine mixture. Now add the tomatoes, salt, sugar, and black pepper. Turn down the heat to low and simmer uncovered for 40 minutes. Do not allow it to boil.

Hard-boil the remaining three eggs and, when they are cooled and peeled, cut them in sixths. Cut the salami and slice the cheese.

About five minutes before the meatballs and sauce are ready, begin to cook the macaroni in the boiling water.

When the 40 minutes have passed, turn off the heat under the tomato sauce and remove the meatballs with a slotted spoon. Preheat the oven to 375°.

When the macaroni is two minutes underdone, drain it and mix it with a little tomato sauce and ½ cup grated cheese.

"Grease" an oven pan with tomato sauce. Place half the macaroni in it. Cover this layer with all of the meatballs, hard-boiled eggs, and salami. Cover this with half of the caciocavalo, a drizzle of tomato sauce, and a sprinkle of grated cheese. Place the rest of the macaroni on top. On this layer arrange the remaining cacio-cavalo, drizzle the remaining tomato sauce, sprinkle the remaining grated cheese and the bread crumbs. Bake at 375° for 15 to 20 minutes and serve immediately.

❧

PASTA 'NCACIATA
(Cheesed Pasta)

This savory dish is prepared everywhere in Sicily. Although ingredients vary from province to province, the result is the same: the pasta tastes as if it were made of cheese.

FOR SIX SERVINGS

1 pound short, tubular macaroni
   such as ziti tagliati or
   penne rigate
⅓ cup hard sheep's milk ricotta
   (ricotta salata), coarsely grated
½ cup locatelli or imported
   pecorino cheese, grated

¼ pound caciocavalo or imported
   provolone, diced
sea salt
black pepper
extra virgin olive oil

FOR THE TOMATO SAUCE

1 28-ounce can Italian
   plum tomatoes
½ medium-sized onion,
   chopped fine
2 tablespoons extra virgin olive oil
1 tablespoon tomato paste,
   dissolved in ¼ cup water

1 teaspoon sugar
1 sprig basil, chopped
sea salt
black pepper

Put up a pot of abundant water with salt and olive oil in which to cook the pasta. Meanwhile, prepare the tomato sauce.

Pass the tomatoes through a food mill fitted with the disk having the smallest holes to remove the seeds. Scrape into the bowl any pulp that has stuck to the bottom side of the mill.

Place the onion and olive oil in a saucepan and sauté at medium heat until the onion becomes clear. Do not brown the onion in any way. Add the tomato paste and cook for a minute or two until it thickens. Add the tomatoes, sugar, salt, pepper, and basil. Cook at low heat for 20 minutes, stirring occasionally. Do not allow it to boil, as the sauce will become bitter.

When the water boils, cook the pasta until it is two minutes underdone. Drain it thoroughly and sauce it in a bowl with just enough sauce to coat it.

Grate and cut the cheeses, leaving them in separate piles. Mix all of the hard ricotta with the pasta.

Choose an oven pan just large enough to accommodate all the pasta. "Grease" the bottom of the pan with some of the sauce. Place half the pasta in the pan with all of the caciocavalo on top. Drizzle some tomato sauce and sprinkle half the grated cheese. Place the rest of the pasta in the pan, drizzle the remaining tomato sauce on top, and the rest of the grated cheese.

Bake at 400° for 45 minutes and serve very hot.

⚜

PASTA CHI SARDI D'ANDREA
(Baked Pasta With Fresh Sardines)

If there is one dish so uniquely Sicilian that it might even be *the* national dish, *pasta chi sardi* is it. The recipe, however, is different in every region, city, town, even neighborhood! Papa Andrea's version, a baked one, is much more delicate and elegant than any other version I have encountered. The use of a fumet as a base for the sauce truly shows the hand of the *monzú*.

Pasta chi sardi is always served to celebrate the feast day of Saint Joseph—March 19. The recipe is for 10 to 12 servings. It can be halved to serve fewer people.

FOR 10 TO 12 SERVINGS

5 pounds fresh sardines,
  1½ ounces each or larger
1 medium-sized onion
  coarsely chopped
4 sprigs Italian parsley
22 peppercorns
2 cups dry white wine
3 cups water
½ pound thin tops of the fennel,
  chopped fine
4 to 6 thick stalks fennel,
  left whole
8 anchovies, melted in a double
  boiler in a little of their oil

½ cup extra virgin olive oil
1 cup (6 ounces) pine nuts,
  coarsely chopped
⅓ cup currants, plumped in
  white wine or water
3 pounds perciatelli pasta
2 tablespoons unflavored
  bread crumbs
1 cup toasted bread crumbs
extra virgin olive oil
sea salt
black pepper
crushed red pepper

The sardines are cleaned in basically the same way as for Sardi a Beccaficu, with the following minor differences: First of all, retain the heads and skeletons. Clean them under cold running water and drain them. Secondly, separate the fillets into the two halves. And thirdly, trim off the tail and dorsal fins, discarding them.

After the sardines are cleaned, put up a large pot of water with salt and a little olive oil in which to cook the pasta.

Now, prepare a fumet of the fish heads and skeletons, which will become the stock for the sauce. In a saucepan well greased with extra virgin olive oil place the sardine heads and skeletons, onion, and peppercorns. Cover and stew at medium heat for 20 minutes, stirring occasionally.

Remove the cover, add white wine, and when the alcohol has evaporated add water. Continue cooking at a gentle boil uncovered for a half hour.

Pour the fumet through a fine mesh strainer into another saucepan, removing all the solids and bones. Mix a few tablespoons of the fumet with the melted anchovies and then mix this thoroughly back into the fumet. Add the half cup of extra virgin olive oil and check for salt and pepper. Keep the sauce covered and warm until ready for use.

When the pasta water boils, cook the perciatelli until it is slightly underdone. Drain it and toss it in a large bowl with the pine nuts, currants, thin fennel tops, and enough of the fish sauce to moisten it.

Preheat the oven to 400°.

Pour a little of the fish sauce in the bottom of an oven pan and add half of the dressed pasta. Arrange the sardine fillets in a single layer and moisten with the sauce. Add the rest of the pasta and fish sauce. Sprinkle the top with untoasted bread crumbs, decorate with the thick whole fennel stalks, and bake at 400° for 35 minutes.

Serve with toasted bread crumbs to sprinkle on top and crushed red pepper to taste.

CONCHIGGUNI CHINI
(Baked Stuffed Shells)

FOR SIX SERVINGS

1 pound conchigliani rigate
(the largest pasta shells)

FOR THE FILLING

homemade or store-bought ricotta
as described in the recipe
for Cannola
1 cup locatelli or imported
pecorino cheese, grated

5 eggs, slightly beaten
¼ cup Italian parsley, chopped
black pepper

FOR THE TOMATO SAUCE

1 28-ounce can Italian
plum tomatoes
1½ tablespoons extra virgin
olive oil
½ medium-sized onion,
chopped fine
¼ pound crimini mushrooms
or ¼ pound white mushrooms
+3 reconstituted dried mushrooms,
chopped

2 tablespoons tomato paste
⅓ cup dry white wine
2 teaspoons sugar
4 scrapes nutmeg
2 sprigs basil, chopped
sea salt
black pepper

Put up a large pot of water with salt and a little olive oil in which to cook the pasta. While waiting for it to boil, prepare the sauce. Pass the contents of the can of tomatoes through a food mill, fitted with the disk having the smallest holes, to remove the seeds. Scrape into the bowl any pulp that has stuck to the bottom side of the mill.

Place the olive oil and onion in a saucepan and sauté at medium heat until the onion turns clear. Do not brown it in any way. Add the mushrooms, salt, and sauté at high heat, stirring to keep the onion or mushrooms from burning.

Dissolve the tomato paste in the white wine. When the mushrooms have given off their liquid and it has almost evaporated, stir in the tomato paste and white wine. Cook for a minute or two until the alcohol has evaporated. Then add the tomatoes, salt, sugar, black pepper, nutmeg, and basil. Simmer at low heat for 20 minutes. Stir from time to time. Do not allow it to boil in any way.

When the pasta water boils, cook the shells until they are two minutes underdone. Handle them gently so they don't tear. Drain and run under cold water until cool. Leave them in a colander to drain while preparing the filling.

Mix the ricotta together with the grated cheese, eggs, black pepper, and parsley. Use a wooden spoon so the cheese doesn't lose all its texture.

"Grease" a large shallow baking pan with a little tomato sauce. Stuff each shell loosely with about 1½ tablespoons of filling. When stuffed, the shells should be mostly closed.

Arrange the shells in neat, tight rows on the baking pan. Drizzle tomato sauce on top. Bake in a preheated 400° oven for 40 minutes. Serve with a bit more tomato sauce and grated cheese on top.

MACCARUNI CHI MULINCIANI 'A FURNU
(Baked Macaroni With Eggplant)

Maccaruni chi mulinciani 'a furnu is a baked version of Pasta alla Norma. It uses the same tomato sauce and cheeses, but it does not use fresh pasta, as it is easily overcooked when baked. Like all baked pastas, last-minute preparation is avoided.

FOUR SERVINGS

1 pound rigatoni pasta or a smaller version such as canneroni or sedani

1 or 2 eggplants weighing a total of 1½ pounds, prepared as for Mulinciani a Palmigiana

1 recipe of the tomato sauce from Pasta alla Norma

⅓-½ pound ricotta salata (hard sheep's ricotta), coarsely grated

Prepare the eggplant and as it nears the end of its pressing time put up a large pot of boiling water with salt and olive oil in which to cook the pasta.

Now prepare the tomato sauce. While it is cooking, continue the eggplant preparation and fry it. Leave the slices of fried eggplant to drain on brown paper until they are ready to use.

When the tomato sauce is ready and the pasta water has boiled, cook the pasta until it is two minutes underdone. Drain it thoroughly, place it in a bowl, and toss it with a little tomato sauce and half the cheese.

Preheat the oven to 400°.

"Grease" the bottom of an oven pan with the tomato sauce. Place half of the pasta in the pan. Cover the pasta with a layer of eggplant, a drizzle of tomato sauce, and a sprinkle of cheese. Add the remaining pasta, then the eggplant, and the rest of the tomato sauce and cheese. Bake in the center of a 400° oven for ½ hour.

'A TUMALA D'ANDREA
(*Rice Bombe*)

A very old Sicilian dish, *'a tumala* was purportedly invented and named after Ibn at-Tumnah, an eleventh-century emir of Catania. The original recipe called for layers of various meats separated by layers of rice and cheese and eggs. Papa Andrea's version is simpler, lighter, and very dramatic in its presentation. In his recipe a wall of rice is molded to a large bowl. The center is filled with macaroni mixed with tomato sauce, cheese, and peas. It is covered with the rice, baked, and de-molded. It is sliced and served with a little tomato sauce and cheese on top.

Tumala is served as a first course for any major holiday from Christmas through Easter.

FOR 8 TO 10 SERVINGS

2 pounds arborio rice

1 pound ziti tagliate
   or penne rigate pasta

5 or 6 eggs

4½ cups locatelli or imported
   pecorino cheese, grated

3 tablespoons extra virgin olive oil

2 28-ounce cans Italian
   plum tomatoes

2 tablespoons tomato paste
   dissolved in ⅓ cup water

4 scrapes nutmeg

3 sprigs basil, chopped

1 tablespoon sugar

½ medium-sized onion,
   chopped fine
¼ pound crimini mushrooms
   or ¼ pound white mushrooms
+3 reconstituted dried mushrooms,
   coarsely chopped
¾ pound chopped veal
¼ pound chopped pork

1 cup shelled peas
enough butter and bread crumbs
   to generously grease and coat
   the inside of a 5-quart stainless
   steel bowl
sea salt
black pepper
extra virgin olive oil

The night before, cook the rice in abundant boiling salted water as one would cook pasta. Drain it well, and when it has cooled somewhat, add four or five beaten eggs, depending on their size, and two cups of the grated cheese. Mix it together very well with a wooden spoon. Place it in a shallow bowl, smooth the top, cover it with a dish towel, and put it in a cool place (not the refrigerator) to set up overnight.

On the day the tumala is to be served, put up a large pot of salted water with a little olive oil in which to cook the pasta. Now prepare the tomato sauce.

Pour the entire contents of the two cans of tomatoes into a food mill, fitted with the disk with the smallest holes, to remove the seeds. Scrape into the bowl any pulp that has stuck to the bottom side of the mill.

In a 3½-quart saucepan place three tablespoons of olive oil and the half onion chopped fine. Set the heat to medium and sauté the onion until it is clear. Do not brown it in any way. Add the mushrooms, turn up the heat to high, and salt. Remember to keep stirring so that nothing sticks to the bottom of the pot. When the liquid that the mushrooms give off is mostly evaporated, add the chopped meat. Keep sautéing and stirring at high heat until the meat is cooked. Break up any clumps with a wooden spoon.

Turn down the heat to medium and add the tomato paste, stirring to coat the mixture in the pot. After about a minute, when the paste begins to thicken, add the tomatoes. Stir well. Add black pepper, salt, sugar, basil, and nutmeg. Cook the sauce at a slow simmer uncovered, stirring occasionally for 40 minutes. Do not allow the sauce to boil. Turn off the heat and warm up the sauce before serving.

When the sauce is ready and the pasta water has boiled, cook the macaroni so that it is slightly underdone. Drain it well and toss it with just enough sauce to coat it. Using a slotted spoon, add ¾ of the solids from the sauce to the pasta, along with ½ cup of the grated cheese and the raw peas. Be sure to note that too much sauce liquid will later leak through and the tumala will crack when it is unmolded.

Now build the rice walls. Grease the 5-quart stainless steel bowl very well with butter. Coat the inside of the bowl thoroughly with bread crumbs all the way up to the top edge. Sprinkle an additional tablespoon of bread crumbs on the bottom of the bowl. Line the bowl with the rice mixture, making a wall ½-inch thick. Press the rice gently but firmly against the bowl with your hand, moistened with water to keep it from sticking. Be sure there are no thin spots. Bring the wall of rice right to the top edge of the bowl.

When the macaroni is room temperature, fill the center with it to 1 inch from the top. Make sure there are no empty spaces.

Cover the top with the remaining rice. Fold over the top edge of the rice wall to meet the top layer of rice so that the tumala is half an inch recessed into the bowl. The top layer must be flat and sealed well all around, as when it is de-molded this will become the bottom and support the whole weight. Brush a beaten egg over the top to ensure a good seal.

Bake the tumala on the center rack of a preheated 400° oven for one hour or until the top is a light golden color.

Upon taking the tumala out of the oven, release the top edge from the bowl, carefully, with a small knife. Let it rest in the bowl for 10 minutes. Then place a serving platter on top of the bowl and turn it over. This step may require four hands. Gently lift off the bowl. If it is stuck, don't panic. Try tapping on the bowl or twisting it gently. Persevere! It will release.

Let it rest for another five minutes and bring it to the table. Slice it there. Serve the slices with a little tomato sauce, grated cheese, and black pepper on top.

"'a Cuccagna" is a mythical land where one can find mountains of pasta and plenty. It has existed in Sicilian folk tales for hundreds of years, and in the courtly literature of the island since the fourteenth century. In the seventeenth and eighteenth centuries the wealthy aristocracy would construct "Cuccagna" for special festive occasions.

This tumala d'Andrea is reminiscent of this other time, when pasta was costly, and every peasant's dream was to eat a mountain of it every day.

I Secondi Piatti di Pisci

(Fish Second Courses)

The coastal regions of Sicily abound in extraordinary fishes of every size and flavor. At least one whole volume could be devoted to Sicilian fish cookery alone.

The traditional cuisine of the mountainous regions, however, is less centered on fresh fish. Prior to the days of the motorcar and refrigeration, the long-distance transport of fresh fish in a Mediterranean climate during summer was difficult and expensive. During the winter, although temperate at the coast, these mountains are snowbound.

The recipes here are typical of the kinds of fish dishes traditional in the Madonie Mountains.

MIRRUZZU SCIUSCIEDDU
(Poached Whiting)

Between 1907 and 1920 my grandmother Carolina gave birth to eleven children, including two sets of twins. She was a beautiful frail woman in delicate health. As was customary at the time, all of her children were delivered at home with the assistance of a midwife. In addition, my grandfather Papa Andrea insisted that there be a doctor in attendance.

Dr. Carini was a fine doctor, a product of the late nineteenth-century tradition where science and art came together in the person of *il dottore*. He was a gentleman of refined tastes, radical social ideas, and eccentric personal habits. The good doctor lived in a house with his offices on the ground floor. His living quarters were stuffed with books on all subjects, personal mementos, and—for his time—an extensive collection of opera and other serious music recordings. He lived with a woman to whom he was not married, and although he was childless, there was a cat whom he treated as a member of the family. The doctor would never accept payment from my grandfather for his obstetric services. His socialistic views sharpened his awareness of the economic conditions affecting new immigrant families. Out of respect for the doctor's goodness and to preserve his own pride, Papa Andrea would cook lunch for the doctor and his family.

The doctor, the mistress, and the cat would sit at the dining room table and while listening to Puccini enjoy their noontime meal. Their favorite second course, especially the cat's, was *mirruzzu sciuscieddu*. Dr. Carini would always remind Papa Andrea that the cat did not prefer lemon. Her fish also needed to be carefully filleted, I suppose, to enhance her table manners.

Sciuscieddu is a wonderful Sicilian word. It refers to a steaming dish, over which one would blow, *shu-shu*, to cool it off.

FOR EVERY TWO SERVINGS

2 whitings, about 1¼ pounds each, whole, gutted, and scaled.

1 lemon, cut in half

⅓ cup extra virgin olive oil

2 medium onions, cut in quarters

coarse sea salt

coarse black pepper

Rinse the fish. Peel and cut the onions and place them together with the fish in a pot. Add the olive oil and enough water to barely cover the fish. Salt and add black pepper.

Cook covered at a temperature just below boiling for 20 minutes.

When it is cooked, transfer each fish to an open bowl. Divide the onion and the liquid. Add lemon juice and additional olive oil to taste. Serve very hot with good bread.

❧

PISCI ARRUSTUTU CHI CACUOCCIULI O FINUCCHI
(Roasted Fish With Artichoke or Fennel)

There is a certain sense of plenty in serving a whole roasted fish. There is also a certain sense of purity. Two of Papa Andrea's ways of preparing a roasted fish were with artichokes or with fennel.

Choose a white meat fish suitable for baking. Allow ¾ of a pound per person. Have it gutted and scaled. Cut off the fins and trim the tail.

If it is to be cooked with artichokes, use one-half of a large artichoke per person and prepare as follows:

Set up a bowl with the juice and rind of one lemon and water. Pass a knife through another lemon before each cut to keep the artichoke from turning black. Peel away the outer leaves until the place where they are light green is reached. Cut about one inch off the top. Pare away the dark green skin from the bottom and the stem. Cut the artichoke in quarters and cut out the choke. Slice the artichoke lengthwise in thin strips so that each piece has some leaves, heart, and stem. Soak the pieces in the lemon water.

If fennel is to be used, slice the bulb and stems very thin. Save the leaves to sprinkle on top after cooking.

Rub the fish with olive oil and salt. Stuff the cavity with the artichokes or fennel. Place it in a well-oiled roasting pan and bake at 450° for 10 minutes per inch at the thickest part of the fish, plus an additional 10 minutes.

Fillet it and serve with the artichoke or fennel, and lemon.

⚜

BRACIOLA 'I PISCI SPATA
(Swordfish Rolls)

In order for this recipe to work, the swordfish must be cut very thin so that it will roll. Have it cut less than ¼-inch thick so that there are 12 pieces to 1½ pounds.

FOR SIX SERVINGS

12 very thin slices of swordfish	12 basil leaves
½ pound swordfish, chopped fine	½ pound caciocavalo or mild
1 small onion, chopped fine	imported provolone cheese,
1 cup extra virgin olive oil	coarsely grated
¼ cup white raisins or sultanas	sea salt
plumped in white wine	black pepper
¼ cup cognac	extra virgin olive oil
4 tablespoons bread crumbs	

Mix the chopped swordfish together with the onion. Heat the olive oil in a skillet and when it is hot add the onion and swordfish. Sauté until the onion begins to brown. Turn off the flame and add the cognac and a sprinkle of salt. Carefully turn the heat back on and when the alcohol has evaporated from the cognac remove the skillet from the heat. Stir in the bread crumbs. Add the black pepper and the raisins.

Wipe the slices of swordfish dry and lay them out on a work surface covered in waxed paper. When the stuffing is cooled, place an equal amount on each slice. Top with a basil leaf and then the cheese. Roll up the slices so the edges meet. Make sure the ends are well closed and secure the rolls with string or toothpicks. Brush each roll with olive oil and cook.

These taste best when cooked outdoors over an open fire or barbecue, but if this is not possible cook them at 450° in the oven for 15 minutes.

SARDI A BECCAFICU
(Stuffed Fresh Sardines)

Beccaficu refers to a variety of small birds categorized as "fig-peckers." They are considered a delicacy. A very poetic Sicilian, somewhere in time, envisioned sardines that were stuffed, rolled, and placed in a pan with their tails in the air, to resemble a cluster of these birds roosting.

FOR SIX TO EIGHT SERVINGS

24 fresh sardines, weighing 1½ ounces or larger, well scaled	4 sprigs Italian parsley zest and juice of one lemon
½ cup extra virgin olive oil	zest and juice of one orange
¾ cup bread crumbs	1 tablespoon sugar
⅓ cup pine nuts	1 dozen bay leaves
⅓ cup currants, plumped in white wine or water	2 onions, sliced 1 orange, sliced
2 tablespoons almond meal	
6 anchovies, melted in a double boiler in some of their olive oil	

First the sardines must be cleaned and filleted. This is actually a simple operation and is accomplished quickly.

Snap off the head by twisting it away from the body. Holding the fish in one hand, slit the belly with the thumbnail of the other and remove the entrails. Continue the slit down the fish and open it like a book. Lay it flat on a work surface with the head end facing you. Slip a thumbnail under the spine and remove it with all the bones. Snap off the spine just below the tail. Leave the tail intact and the two fillets connected. Rinse them under cold running water to clean and remove any loose bone. Leave the skin on.

As each sardine is cleaned, place it on a platter tilted so that the liquid drains into the sink.

While the sardines are draining, prepare the stuffing. In a heavy 9-inch skillet put 2 tablespoons of the olive oil and the bread crumbs. Toast them at low heat until they are a rich brown color. Keep the bread crumbs moving. Nothing will happen at first, but then the browning will occur quickly.

Add the melted anchovies and mix into the bread crumbs thoroughly. Add the almond meal, pine nuts, and currants. Moisten with an additional two tablespoons of olive oil and mix well. Remove from the stove and pour the contents into a bowl.

When the mixture has cooled somewhat, mix in the orange and lemon zest chopped fine, the parsley, and the sugar.

Cover a countertop with waxed paper. Lay out the sardines in neat rows with the skin side down and the tail facing away from you. Place an equal amount of stuffing on each sardine.

Grease an 8-inch-square oven pan with a little olive oil. Place the bay leaves on the bottom. Preheat the oven to 375°.

Roll up each sardine toward the tail, keeping the stuffing inside. After rolling each one, place it in the pan with a slice of onion between it and the next and with the tail up in the air. Fit them tightly into the pan so they do not unroll. Salt and pepper to taste. Pour the remaining olive oil over the top and bake at 375° for 45 minutes.

Upon removal from the oven, add the lemon juice and orange juice. When it is room temperature refrigerate, covered, until slightly chilled. Serve the dish in the same pan in which it was cooked, decorated with sliced orange.

GAMBEREDDI CU MUGGHIU
(Shrimp With "Mugghiu" Sauce)

Shrimp cooked and sauced in this manner are delicious on a hot summer night, as the cooking time is short, keeping the kitchen cool.

Mugghiu is a simple sauce of two parts extra virgin olive oil and one part lemon juice beaten together with sea salt and fresh or dried oregano to taste.

Use medium or large shrimp. Allow ½ pound of shrimp per person. Cook them in boiling water for 2 minutes. Drain the shrimp and serve with the shells from a large bowl. Provide each person with a ramekin of mugghiu in which to dip the shrimp, as they are peeled.

SARDI A CAMMINEDDU
(Fire-Roasted Sardines)

Scale and gut the fresh sardines. Brush them with extra virgin olive oil. Then simply roast them directly over the coals for about eight minutes. Serve moistened with mugghiu.

Eat them by holding the fish firmly by the head and tail and gently sucking away the fillets.

❧

CALAMARI CHINI A GHIOTTA
(Stuffed Squid, Glutton's Style)

In Sicilian cooking the addition of tomatoes, olives, and potatoes is classified as "glutton's style." In this case it is a bit of a joke, however, since the delicacy of the stuffing and the lightness of the sauce creates a dish far from anything related to the seven deadly sins.

FOR SIX SERVINGS

24 squid, about 2 1/2 pounds, each one 5 inches long and as wide as possible

3/4 cup unflavored bread crumbs

16 black oil-cured olives, pitted and chopped very fine

2 tablespoons very finely chopped onion

2 sprigs Italian parsley, chopped fine

1/2 cup extra virgin olive oil

3 cloves garlic, whole and peeled

1/3 cup sun-dried tomato paste or 1/2 cup tomato paste

1 cup dry white wine

1 cup water

2 pounds white potatoes, peeled and cut in 1-inch cubes

sea salt

black pepper

crushed red pepper

Clean the squid as described in the recipe for Insalata 'i Calamari. Do not, however, cut the sacs or the tentacles.

While the squid is in its final soak, peel and cut the potatoes. Soak the potatoes in a separate bowl of cold water.

Place the bread crumbs in another bowl. Drain the tentacles and chop them very fine. Add them to the bread crumbs along with the onions, olives, parsley, and a few grindings of black pepper. Mix together thoroughly.

Drain the sacs and pat them dry. Stuff each one to three-quarters full with the stuffing. The squid will shrink in cooking, so if they are stuffed too full or too tightly they will crack open.

If you find the top opening of the squid too small to stuff easily or in any way uncooperative, try using a small cylinder like an apple corer or a cannoli form or even a sausage stuffing attachment to hold it open. Once you have found a system that works for you, the task becomes simple.

Close the end of each sac securely with a toothpick. Gently squeeze the sac to distribute the stuffing evenly. If there is a small amount of stuffing left over, add it later to the sauce.

In a large, heavy skillet place the olive oil and the garlic and crushed red pepper to taste. Turn the heat on low and sauté the garlic until it begins to take color on all sides. Remove it and discard. Add the tomato paste and mix it well into the oil with a wooden spoon. Turn off the heat to avoid splattering or a fire and stir in the white wine. Carefully turn the heat back on and cook for a few minutes until the alcohol has evaporated. Stir in the water and when the sauce is well mixed add the remaining stuffing, if any.

Add the drained potatoes and turn them in the sauce. Salt.

Now add the stuffed squid so that they are in one layer and at least partially submerged in the sauce. Cover, turn down the heat to low, and cook at a simmer for 40 minutes. Turn the squid once or twice during this time.

When it is cooked, transfer the squid to a warmed serving platter and remove the toothpicks. Arrange the potatoes on the platter. Reduce the sauce, if necessary, and pour it over the top.

FUNCI CHINI
Stuffed Mushrooms

❧

ARANCI E FINUCCHI 'NINSALATA
Orange and Fennel Salad

❧

CAPUNATINA
Eggplant and Olive Salad

❧

BRACIOLA
Sicilian Stuffed Beef Cutlets

❧

SALAMI 'I TUNNU 'NSTEMPERATA
Salame of Tuna in Stemperata

SARDI A BECCAFICU
Stuffed Fresh Sardines

&

L'OVA 'NCAMISSA
Egg-in-a-Shirt Soup

&

PASTA CU SPARACEDDU ARRIMINATU
Pasta With Cauliflower

&

'A TUMALA D'ANDREA
Rice Bombe

&

PASTA ALLA NORMA
Fresh Pasta With Eggplant

COPPA 'I TRI COLORI
Three Flavors in a Cup

❧

MINNI 'I VIRGINI
Virgin's Breasts

❧

BISCOTTI 'I PAN 'I SPAGNA
Anisette Toast

❧

ACCEDDU CU L'OVA
Easter Cakes

❧

MELUNI 'NGHIACHIATA
Frozen Melon

FRAGULI SUTTU SPIRITU E BISCOTTI 'I FINUCCHI

Strawberries Soaked in Sweet Vermouth with Fennel Seed Cookies

TUNNINA CHI CIPPUDDI
(Tuna With Onions)

The meatlike quality of fresh tuna lends itself well to this quickly prepared, delicious dish.

FOR FOUR SERVINGS

4 tuna steaks, cut ½-inch thick

2 medium-sized onions, sliced thin

4 fresh Roma or Italian
    plum tomatoes

3 sprigs Italian parsley, chopped

½ cup white wine

¼ cup extra virgin olive oil

flour for dusting

sea salt

black pepper

Cut the tomatoes in half lengthwise and remove the seed pod with a small spoon. Chop the remaining part of the tomato fine. Peel and slice the onion.

Heat 2 tablespoons of the olive oil in a skillet large enough to later accommodate the fish in one layer. Place the onions and tomatoes in the pan. Salt. Sauté at medium heat. Use a wooden spatula to distribute the tomato. When the onion turns clear, it is done. Remove from pan and place on a plate.

Pat the tuna steaks dry and lightly dust each one with flour. Place the remaining two tablespoons of olive oil in the pan and turn up the heat to high. When the oil is hot, slip in the tuna steaks and brown them on all sides. Return the onion mixture to the pan and when it is hot, turn off the fire and add the white wine. Carefully turn the heat back on and cook for a few minutes until the alcohol has evaporated, turning the fish once during this time.

Turn down the heat to low, adding parsley and black pepper. Cover and gently cook for 10 to 15 minutes.

When the fish is cooked, arrange it on a warmed serving platter with the onion and tomato topping.

I Secondi Piatti di Carne

(Meat Second Courses)

$\mathscr{E}$arly one morning in 1897, in a small Sicilian city named Polizzi Generosa, my grandfather Andrea Coco was summoned by his master, Baron Rampolla. Gesturing Andrea closer with his index finger, the Baron, speaking in the familiar form, as to a small child, says, "Listen, Andrea, tonight I am having special guests for dinner and I want you to cook something very special for them." Andrea, eyes lowered in reverence, voices compliance in his most courteous and formal manner. As the baron takes his leave, walking away, Andrea, head chef of this baronial estate, says to himself, "That son-of-a-————! Don't I *always* cook him something special? Let's see just how special these important people and their tastes really are."

Andrea returns to the kitchen and sends two of his staff into the countryside to catch field mice. When they return from the hunt with their catch, Andrea dresses the creatures and fillets the meat. He soaks the fillets in milk with a little cinnamon all day. Then he carefully pounds the meat and makes it into meat rolls, called *spiteddi*.

The evening arrives. The estate is aglow with candlelight. The courtyard rings with the sound of arriving carriages. Guests, dressed in their splendid evening clothes, are escorted into the house by servants in livery carrying candelabra.

The dinner begins with an assortment of antipasti, followed by two pasta courses, one of them baked, and a fish course. And then, just before the roast, the "specialty" of the chef is served.

So the mice go into the dining room. After a while one of the maids returns to the kitchen in tears. She says to Andrea, "They want to see you in the dining room. Blessed Virgin in Heaven, they must know everything! They will kill you!"

Andrea calms her down, but proceeds to the dining room with a certain amount of apprehension. He knocks on the door. He is admitted. The Baron says, "Ah, Andrea! Come forward!" indicating so with his index finger. "Tell me, what was this meat you served us?"

Before Andrea can respond, one of the guests says, "It was pork." Another says, "Pork? Oh, no, no. It was rabbit, of course." Another says, "Veal." Still another says, "You are all mad. It was chicken." And so it went, all around the table, until finally the Baron concludes, ". . . because we have never tasted a meat so delicious. What was it?" With the greatest courtesy, Andrea responds, "If you please, my lords and ladies, it was my touch."

You see, he didn't need to rub their noses in it. They had already eaten the mice and enjoyed them. The Baron and his guests then cheered, "Bravo! Bravo, Andrea!"

SPITEDDI
(Meat Rolls)

These lovely rollentines are easy to prepare and produce a result that seems much more complicated than it actually is. The cutlets are cut from the sirloin tip of the beef, the same part as veal cutlets are cut from the calf. In markets which cater to a Hispanic clientele they are called *milanesa*. Choose slices that are broad, thin, and very lean.

FOR FOUR SERVINGS

8 beef cutlets weighing about 2 pounds	½ cup dry white wine
	¼ cup shelled peas
1⅓ cups bread crumbs	8 thin slices caciocavalo or
½ cup chopped green olives	provolone cheese
¼ cup +2 tablespoons extra virgin olive oil	sea salt
	black pepper
2 cloves garlic, peeled and whole	

Lay out the meat on waxed paper on a work surface. Salt each piece. Toast the bread crumbs in 2 tablespoons of the olive oil until they are a rich brown color. Place them into a bowl.

Pit and chop the olives and add them to the bread crumbs. When the bread crumbs are cool, spread this mixture of olive and bread crumbs evenly on each cutlet and place a slice of cheese in the center. Roll them up using toothpicks or string to hold them together.

In a skillet large enough to hold the rolls in one layer place the remaining olive oil and garlic. Sauté the garlic until it is a light golden color and discard it. Brown the rolls thoroughly on all sides at high heat. Turn down the heat, add the white wine and black pepper. Turn them once and pepper the other side. When the alcohol has evaporated, add ¼ cup water down the side of the skillet. Turn the heat to low, place on a cover askew, and cook for 45 minutes to an hour. Check from time to time to see if more water is required. After 35 minutes, add the peas.

When ready, relocate the spiteddi and peas to a heated platter. Reduce the sauce if necessary, pour over the spiteddi, and serve.

BRACIOLA

(Sicilian Stuffed Beef Cutlets)

Braciola is served everywhere in Sicily. In some places it is called *fasumagru*, which probably comes from the French *faux maigre*, meaning "false lean."

This version is from Papa Andrea and very tasty. Traditionally, braciola is served after the pasta and before the main meat course. As a proper second course, however, it is pleasing to serve individual portions sliced, delicately sauced, and accompanied by steamed carrots.

The recipe here serves four, but simple multiplication of the ingredients can increase the yield to any number.

FOR FOUR SERVINGS

4 beef cutlets (also called milanesa), cut from the sirloin tip, pounded very flat and wide, weighing about ¼ pound each

2 ounces caciocavalo or provolone cheese, diced

1¼-inch slice Sicilian or Italian hard salami (about 2 ounces), diced

½ pound ground veal

1 egg, beaten

2 eggs, hard-boiled and cut in half lengthwise

extra virgin olive oil

sea salt

black pepper

FOR THE TOMATO SAUCE

1 28-ounce can Italian plum tomatoes

½ medium-sized onion, chopped fine

2 tablespoons extra virgin olive oil

2 tablespoons tomato paste dissolved in ⅓ cup water

1 teaspoon sugar

1 sprig basil

sea salt

black pepper

Pierce the eggshells to keep them from cracking and hard-boil the eggs.

Meanwhile, prepare the tomato sauce. Pass the tomatoes through a food mill, fitted with the disk with the smallest holes, to remove the seeds. Scrape into the bowl any pulp that has stuck to the bottom side of the mill.

Place the olive oil and onion in a 3½-quart saucepan. Sauté at medium heat. When the onion turns clear, add the tomato paste. Cook for about one minute until it thickens. Add the tomatoes, sugar, salt, pepper, and basil. Cook at a very low heat. Do not allow the sauce to boil.

Prepare the stuffing. Mix the veal, cheese, salami, and beaten egg together in a bowl. Salt and pepper. Remember that both the cheese and salami are salty, so adjust for that.

Place each cutlet on a work surface covered with waxed paper. Place equal amounts of stuffing on each cutlet. Place half of a hard-boiled egg on each. Roll up the cutlets, slightly overlapping the edge, and tie them into neat, closed packages.

Heat two tablespoons of olive oil in a skillet on high heat. When it is hot, brown each braciola on all sides. Then place them in the tomato sauce and cook gently for one hour. Serve as previously suggested.

COSCIA 'I AGNEDDU ARRUSTUTU
CHI PATATI
(Roast Leg of Lamb With Potatoes)

Spring lamb has a most delicate and delicious flavor. The season should not pass without cooking it at least once. Papa Andrea always roasted it with onions and rosemary, an excellent complement to its delicacy.

FOR EIGHT TO TEN SERVINGS

1 8-pound leg of lamb, with the bone in	6 medium-sized russet potatoes
2 medium-sized onions	1 cup dry white wine
3 sprigs fresh rosemary	sea salt
	black pepper

Chop the onions very fine. Place them in a bowl and mix with the three sprigs of fresh rosemary, chopped fine, and black pepper.

Salt the lamb on all sides. Preheat the oven to 375°.

Place the lamb on a roasting rack in an oven pan. Crust the onions and rosemary on top. Roast the lamb in the top third of the oven for 2 hours, 40 minutes, which is 20 minutes to the pound.

Peel and cut the potatoes in sixths. Let them soak in cold, salted water.

After the lamb has roasted for one hour, drain the potatoes and add them to the bottom of the pan. Turn them from time to time.

When the onions are very dark brown—in fact, burned—pour the white wine over the roast.

When the lamb is ready, let it rest for 10 minutes before carving.

COSCIA 'I MAIALI ARRUSTUTU
(Roast Loin of Pork)

Sliced very thin and served at room temperature, this pork loin roast makes an excellent part of a buffet. The preparation is similar to that of Coscia 'i Agneddu Arrustutu with certain differences.

Choose a boned pork loin roast at about four ounces per serving. Salt it on all sides and cover the top with coarse ground pepper. Crust enough finely chopped onions on top to generously cover it.

Roast it on a roasting rack in a preheated 375° oven for 30 minutes to the pound plus an additional 30 minutes.

When the onions are very dark brown—in fact, burned—baste it with white wine, being careful not to disturb the onions.

When the roast is room temperature, slice it very thin and arrange it on a serving platter, leaving behind any of the topping which has fallen off. In fact, there may not be much of the onions left, but the flavor will be well into the meat. Because of this flavor, a sauce is unnecessary.

AGNEDDU CARTOCIATU
(Leg of Lamb Cooked in Paper)

When the spring lamb season has passed, this is an excellent way to prepare leg of lamb. The leg is boned, stuffed, sewn together, and wrapped in paper. It is cooked slowly in a covered pot until quite tender.

Have the leg boned and slightly butterflied so that the stuffing will fit inside the cavity left by removal of the bone. When sewing the lamb back together, try to maintain its original shape.

FOR EIGHT SERVINGS

1 6-pound leg of lamb,
  boned and butterflied
1 medium-sized onion,
  chopped fine
½ pound crimini mushrooms
  or white mushrooms, chopped
½ ounce dried porcini
  mushrooms
1½ cups shelled peas
1 lamb liver or
½ pound calf's liver, cut into
  very small cubes
¼ pound prosciutto in one slice,
  cut into small cubes

3 tablespoons extra virgin olive oil
3 slices Italian bread, ¾ inch thick,
  without the crust, soaked in
  milk and squeezed of
  excess liquid.
1 cup locatelli or imported
  pecorino cheese
4 eggs
2 tablespoons butter
1 tablespoon extra virgin olive oil
sea salt
black pepper

Place the dried porcini in a small bowl. Pour a cup and a half of boiling water over them. Cover and let them reconstitute for about five minutes.

Transfer the porcini by fork to a plate, leaving behind the dirt and small stones. Strain the liquid through a fine sieve and save for use in the cooking. Chop the porcini.

Place 3 tablespoons of olive oil and the onion in a skillet on medium heat. When the onion turns clear, add the mushrooms, liver, prosciutto, and peas. Salt and cook for about 15 minutes until all the liquid is evaporated. Transfer the mixture to a bowl.

When it is completely cooled, add the bread, cheese, beaten eggs, and black pepper. Mix it together very well, being careful not to mash the peas.

Stuff the lamb with the mixture, fold it over, and sew it together. Try to reassemble it in its original shape. Do not leave any holes or gaps. Wrap the lamb in oiled kitchen parchment. Secure it in place with strong cotton string.

Melt 2 tablespoons butter and 1 tablespoon olive oil in a pot large enough to hold the meat. When the butter is melted, place the package in the pot. Cover and cook at medium low heat for ½ hour to the pound of lamb. If the butter starts to crackle, pour some of the mushroom liquid into the bottom of the pot. Add more when necessary.

When it is cooked, remove the package from the pot and let it rest for 10 minutes before unwrapping.

Cut it in thick slices and serve with the pan juices.

ARRUSTUCIDDU 'I AGNEDDU
(*Lamb Shish Kabab*)

In style, *arrustuciddu 'i agneddu* is North African, but the marinade is distinctly Sicilian. Use skewers that are long enough to span the width of your barbecue and that have flat blades to better hold the meat and vegetables. Good sources for this type of skewer are stores which sell Middle Eastern or Armenian products.

FOR FOUR SERVINGS

2 pounds lamb, cut from the leg or shoulder in 16 large shish-kabab-style pieces

1 head fennel, cut in half and separated

2 medium-sized onions, cut in quarters and separated

2 small bell peppers, cut in quarters

6 Roma or small, round tomatoes, halved

12 white or oyster mushrooms

FOR THE MARINADE

5 anchovies, melted in a little of their oil in a double boiler

¼ cup red wine vinegar

¼ cup marsala

¼ cup extra virgin olive oil

3 cloves garlic, pressed

2 sprigs rosemary, chopped

2 sprigs mint, chopped

¼ cup water

black pepper

Whisk the marinade together. Marinate the lamb for two hours, covered in a cool place unrefrigerated.

Arrange the lamb and vegetables on the skewers, bracketing the meat with onion and fennel.

Cook directly over the coals. Use some mint sprigs tied together to make a brush. Baste the skewers with the marinade.

To serve this dish accompanied by rice pilaf (Risu Pilau) may be crossing the Mediterranean a bit, but I believe it to be appropriate.

PUNTA 'I PETTU CHINI
(Stuffed Breast of Veal)

This recipe for *punta 'i pettu chini* is adapted from one attributed to the great Sicilian artist, ceramicist, and culturalist Giovanni de Simone. It is the most extraordinary stuffed breast of veal I have ever tasted.

If you are not deft at boning and cutting a pocket in the veal, ask your butcher to do it for you. Beet greens, used in this recipe, are usually sold only with the beets attached. Pick good, green, leafy ones and serve the beets themselves at a different meal.

FOR SIX TO EIGHT SERVINGS

½ of 1 side breast of veal
(approximately 5½ pounds),
boned and cut with a pocket

1 pound veal sweetbreads

1 pound beet greens

1 cup locatelli or imported
pecorino cheese, grated

3 slices Italian bread, ¾ inch thick,
without crust, soaked in milk
and squeezed of excess liquid.

¼ pound green olives

½ cup pine nuts (3 ounces)

2 1-ounce slices pancetta

2 eggs

4 tablespoons butter

1 tablespoon extra virgin olive oil

1 cup dry white wine

Soak the sweetbreads in warm water for 15 minutes in order to loosen the skin. Then pull off the skin and brown them in 2 tablespoons butter. Transfer them to a bowl.

Clean the beet greens in a sink filled with cold water. Cut off the thick stems and sauté them in the same skillet which was used to brown the sweetbreads. When they are soft, add them to the bowl.

Add the bread to the mixture. Chop the olives and pine nuts together and add them to the mixture, along with the grated cheese and eggs. Chop the pancetta into small dice and add it as well. Mix it all together into a smooth, homogeneous mixture.

When it is completely cooled, stuff it loosely into the pocket. Sew the pocket shut with needle and thread. Make sure it is well sealed.

Place the remaining butter and olive oil in a pan which can be used on top of the stove as well as in the oven. Turn the heat to high and when the butter has melted, brown the stuffed breast of veal on all sides. Bathe it in the white wine.

Salt and add pepper.

Bake uncovered at 375° for 1½ hours. Let it rest for 15 minutes, then cut in slices and serve.

❧

RUGNUNI CHI PATATI
(Kidneys and Potatoes)

When I was in grade school, nearly everyone went home for lunch. My grandfather Papa Andrea would cook exquisite meals for himself, my grandmother, and me. These took the form of hearty soups or stews that were ready when I arrived home or, depending on the season, salads or dishes that were prepared quickly. From time to time we would eat veal kidneys sautéed with potatoes. The dish was one of my favorites and I was always delighted to find it on my plate.

In general, these lunches were considerably different from the more Italian-American or American fare consumed by my classmates. During the comparison of lunches, a sometimes postprandial schoolyard activity, the disclosure that my lunch had been kidneys produced only guttural sounds from my classmates. But I really enjoyed eating them!

Veal kidneys are delicate in flavor and do not require blanching or braising in advance as beef kidneys do.

FOR FOUR SERVINGS

2 veal kidneys	3 sprigs Italian parsley, chopped fine
2 pounds potatoes	sea salt
¾ cup extra virgin olive oil	black pepper

Cut the kidneys in pieces about the size of a small mushroom cap. While doing this, cut away all of the white fat in the center of the kidney and discard it.

Peel the potatoes and cut them into pieces slightly larger than the kidneys.

Place ½ cup of the olive oil in a large, well-cured skillet. Turn the heat to medium and when the skillet is hot add the potatoes and salt. Turn them gently in the pan with a spatula to prevent sticking or burning. Turn the heat to high and fry them for about 12 minutes until they are well browned and crispy. Remove the potatoes and place them on a plate near the stove to keep warm.

Place the remaining ¼ cup of olive oil in the skillet. When it is hot, add the kidneys and salt. Sauté at high heat for five minutes. Keep them moving to avoid sticking.

Return the potatoes to the skillet and gently mix them together with the kidneys. Continue cooking for a minute or two until the potatoes are hot.

Transfer to a heated serving platter. Sprinkle with parsley and black pepper.

FICATEDDI CA MARSALA
(Chicken Livers Marsala)

FOR FOUR SERVINGS

1 pound fresh chicken livers	³/₄ cup marsala
2 large onions, sliced	sea salt
2 tablespoons butter	black pepper
1 tablespoon olive oil	chopped Italian parsley

Melt the butter with the olive oil in a skillet. Add the onion and cook slowly until it is a rich golden color.

Turn up the heat and add the chicken livers. Keep them moving to prevent sticking. Cook them for five minutes at high heat. Carefully add the marsala, salt, and black pepper. Continue cooking until the marsala begins to thicken.

Transfer to a warmed platter. Garnish with the chopped parsley and serve.

QUAGGHIA 'N PIGNATA
(Pan-Roasted Quail)

FOR FOUR SERVINGS

8 quail	2 tablespoons extra virgin olive oil
8 slices pancetta, very thin	1 cup dry white wine
¹/₄ cup cognac	sea salt
4 sprigs fresh rosemary	black pepper
2 tablespoons butter	

Wash the quail in cold running water and leave them on a tilted platter or upright in a colander to drain for 10 minutes.

Then stuff each quail with a slice of pancetta, several rosemary leaves, and 2 teaspoonfuls of cognac. Place them on a platter on their side so the cognac does not run out. Heat the butter and olive oil in a heavy skillet large enough to accommodate the quail in one layer. When the butter stops foaming, brown the quail thoroughly on all sides at high heat. Turn off the heat to avoid an accidental fire, add any leftover cognac and the white wine. Turn the heat back on, add salt and black pepper. Turn the quail once while the wine bubbles and the alcohol evaporates.

Turn down the heat very low and cover with the lid slightly askew. Cook for 35 to 40 minutes. Check from time to time to make sure the quail aren't sticking and that there is enough liquid. If water does need to be added, pour it down the side of the pan, not over the quail.

When the quail are cooked, transfer them to a heated platter. Reduce the sauce until it is quite thick and smooth and pour it over the top. Serve very hot.

GADDINA CATANISI
(Catania-Style Chicken)

I have chosen to include *gaddina catanisi* here because of its strong North African influence. It exemplifies the diversity of Sicily's culinary history.

Cut a 3½ to 4-pound chicken into eight parts. Sprinkle each part with salt, fresh rosemary and marjoram, chopped garlic to taste, and a good three scrapes of nutmeg.

Choose a pan that will accommodate the chicken in one layer and can be used on top of the stove as well as in the oven. Place a small amount of extra virgin olive oil in the pan, turn heat to high, and brown the chicken.

When the chicken is well browned on all sides, add a bunch of scallions, chopped (use only the white ends), one cup of orange juice from the most bitter oranges available, pepper, and 4 tablespoons cognac. Transfer to a preheated oven at 375°. Bake for 1¼ hours. Baste the chicken with the pan juices from time to time. When cooked, serve it in the pan in which it was baked.

GADDINA CIPPUDATA
(Chicken With Smothered Onions)

This onion sauce is usually used in Sicilian fish dishes. Papa Andrea used it for chicken. His addition of mushrooms gives *gaddina cippudata* a more rustic, mountain flavor.

FOR FOUR SERVINGS

1 3½-4-pound chicken, cut into 8 pieces	5 scrapes nutmeg
	sea salt
2 pounds onions, chopped fine	black pepper
½ pound crimini or white button mushrooms, cleaned	a mixture of ½ flour, ½ cornstarch for dusting
2 tablespoons extra virgin olive oil	4 sprigs Italian parsley, chopped
1 cup dry white wine	

Wash off the chicken and pat it dry. Salt each piece. Place the olive oil in a skillet large enough to accommodate the chicken in one layer. Turn heat to medium and while the oil is heating dust each piece of chicken with the flour-cornstarch mixture.

When the oil is hot, brown the chicken at high heat on all sides. Be careful not to burn it, as the cornstarch can increase this possibility. When the chicken is browned, transfer it to a plate.

Pour most of the fat out of the skillet, leaving just enough to barely coat the bottom of the pan. Add the chopped onion and sauté at medium heat until it is a rich golden brown.

Return the chicken to the pan. When it is hot, add the white wine, salt, pepper, and nutmeg. Scrape the bottom of the pot and turn the chicken one time in the wine. Cook for several minutes until the alcohol has evaporated.

When the alcohol has evaporated, use a wooden spatula to place the onion on top of the chicken. Turn down the heat to low, cover, and simmer for 1¼ hours. Check it from time to time to make sure there is enough liquid. If necessary, add water down the side of the pan, not over the chicken.

After ¾ hour of cooking time, add the mushrooms, salt, and submerge them as best as possible into the sauce.

When the chicken is cooked, transfer it and the mushrooms to a warmed serving platter. Reduce the sauce if necessary. Pour it over the chicken. Sprinkle with chopped parsley.

CAPUNI CHINI 'I CASTAGNE
(*Roasted Capon Stuffed With Chestnuts*)

A capon is a castrated rooster. This very old tradition turns an extra rooster that could create discord in the henhouse into an excellent, plump, roasting fowl. Capons are dressed in mid-December, making them available for Christmas.

Chestnuts are plentiful in the Madonie Mountains in Sicily. They are harvested in the autumn, and Christmastime is the height of their season.

Papa Andrea always roasted capons stuffed with chestnuts for Christmas dinner.

FOR EIGHT SERVINGS

1 9-pound capon, including the neck, liver, heart, and gizzard

2 ½ pounds chestnuts
or 30 ounces chestnuts, jarred
or canned whole, cooked

¾ to 1 cup locatelli or imported pecorino cheese, grated

4 eggs

½ pound crimini mushrooms
or ½ pound white mushrooms
and several reconstituted
dried mushrooms

1 ½ cups toasted bread crumbs

3 tablespoons extra virgin olive oil

¼ cup cognac

⅓ pound pancetta

1 cup dry white wine

sea salt

black pepper

ADDITIONAL INGREDIENTS FOR THE GRAVY

1 carrot, cut in thirds

2 stalks celery, cut in thirds

1 medium-sized onion, cut in quarters

1 handful Italian parsley

1 quart water

1 teaspoon coarse sea salt

12 peppercorns

3 tablespoons flour

½ cup dry white wine

2 tablespoons cognac

Preparing fresh chestnuts for this stuffing is very labor-intensive. There is, however, no difference in the taste when canned ones are used instead. If the canned ones are unavailable to you, or if you have a chestnut harvest of your own, observe the following process.

With a small, sharp, pointed knife, incise a cross on the rounded side of each chestnut. This is done so that they will not explode while roasting. Roast the chestnuts in a 375° oven for 10 minutes. When they are cool enough to handle, shell them.

Very often the inner shell sticks to the nut. In order to remove the inner shell, blanch the chestnuts in boiling water for two minutes. Run them under cold water to cool them quickly and remove this inner shell. There is no harm done if any of the chestnuts break, but all of this inner shell must be removed.

Now continue to cook the chestnuts either in boiling water or steam for 30 to 40 minutes until they are tender. Drain them thoroughly. The preparation up to this point can be done the day before they are to be used.

If you are using canned chestnuts, the only preparation is that they be drained thoroughly.

The crop of the capon is stuffed with mushrooms and bread crumbs to offer some diversity. Clean the mushrooms with a mushroom brush. Do not soak them. If dried mushrooms are used, reconstitute them.

Slice the mushrooms in sixths or eighths. Place the olive oil in a skillet on high heat until it is almost smoking. Add the mushrooms. Salt. Sauté until their liquid has begun to evaporate. Turn off the heat to avoid splattering or a fire and add ¼ cup of cognac. Carefully turn the heat back on and cook until the alcohol has evaporated and the remaining liquid begins to thicken. Turn off the heat and add the toasted bread crumbs, mixing them well into the contents of the skillet. Turn the mixture out into a bowl. When it is cooled, add 1 beaten egg.

Meanwhile, prepare the capon for stuffing. Remove the two pieces of fat from either side of the opening of the cavity. Place this fat in a small pot on very low heat to render. Be sure it doesn't burn. This rendered fat will be used later in the gravy.

Rinse the capon thoroughly under running water. Pat the outside dry and stuff the inside with a wad of paper towels or a dish towel to dry it as well.

While the capon is drying, preheat the oven to 375° and prepare the chestnut stuffing. Place the cooked chestnuts in a bowl and mash them to a lumpy consistency. Mix in the grated cheese, 3 beaten eggs, and black pepper.

Remove the towels from inside the bird, turn it over to breast down, and stuff the crop with the mushroom stuffing. Sew this opening shut with needle and thread.

Turn the bird over breast up. Arrange the ends of the legs in that band of skin. If it is not provided, tie them together. Stuff the main cavity with the chestnut stuffing. Transfer the capon onto a roasting rack in an oven pan.

If you do not own a roasting rack, take about a foot of heavy-duty aluminum foil, squeeze it into the shape of a rolling pin, and join the ends to form a doughnut. Perhaps you will need two of these, but in any case, it will serve the same purpose as a roasting rack—to keep the capon out of the pan juices.

Cover the top of the capon with pancetta. Make sure to put a piece over the opening where the stuffing is. Place the bird in the oven. Cook it for three hours or 20 minutes to the pound.

When the pancetta has become well done, remove it, for it has given up all of its flavor. At this point, baste the capon with the white wine. If you feel it is necessary later on to baste it again, use water.

As soon as the capon is placed in the oven to begin roasting, prepare the stock for the gravy. Place the neck, liver, heart, giblets, carrot, celery, onion, parsley, salt, and peppercorns in a pot with one quart cold water. Bring it slowly to a boil, skimming off any scum which rises to the top. When it boils, turn down the heat, cover, and simmer for one-half hour. Strain the stock through a fine mesh strainer and degrease it using your favorite method. Reserve three cups of the degreased stock for the gravy.

When the capon is ready, place it on a heated serving platter in a warm place to rest for 30 minutes. This is done so that the juices which have collected in the cavity during the cooking return to the meat. While the capon is resting, prepare the gravy.

Remove and degrease the pan juices. If anything has stuck to the bottom of the pan, use a little water and a spatula over low heat to scrape these bits free.

Place 3 tablespoons of the rendered fat in a heavy skillet. Set heat to low. When the fat is hot, but by no means smoking, sprinkle in the flour. Whisk the flour and fat into a roux. Cook until it is a rich brown color. Whisk constantly and do not allow it to burn.

Add the white wine a little at a time, whisking it well into the roux to keep a smooth consistency. Be sure that all of the alcohol has evaporated or there will be a bitter finish in the gravy. (If in the end this is the case, the gravy may be saved by adding a little sugar and allowing it to boil freely for a minute or two.)

Now whisk in the pan juices, again a little at a time. Finally, whisk in the stock in the same manner, but you will notice at some point that the danger of lumps has passed.

Pour the gravy into a saucepan. Check the salt and pepper and add two tablespoons of cognac. Let it simmer uncovered until after the capon has rested and been carved. Place it in a gravy boat and bring it, together with the capon, to the table.

PUPETTI

(Meatballs)

FOR FOUR SERVINGS

³/₄ pound ground veal

¹/₄ pound ground pork

3 slices Italian bread without
the crust, soaked in milk and
squeezed of excess liquid

2 eggs

¹/₄ cup locatelli or imported
pecorino cheese, grated

2 cloves garlic, whole and peeled

extra virgin olive oil for frying

black pepper

Mix the veal, pork, bread, cheese, eggs, and black pepper thoroughly in a bowl. The best way to accomplish this is with your hand.

Form the mixture into oval-shaped meatballs that will fit in the palm of your hand, about 2 inches long and 1 inch thick.

Place the oil and garlic in a heavy skillet. When the oil is hot, cook the meatballs at medium high heat until they are well browned on the outside and cooked through. While cooking the meatballs, discard the garlic when it begins to turn brown.

Drain the meatballs on brown paper. Serve immediately, accompanied by a mixed green salad.

I Contorni

(Accompaniments)

*I*n translation, *contorno* means "edge, border, outline, or contour." In Sicilian culinary terms, the word refers to vegetable accompaniments that fill the edges of the plate and border the second course. Sometimes they are served as a separate course following the outline of the meal and the contour of one's palate, appetite, and tradition.

⚜

'A SCAROLA

(Escarole)

My childhood was filled with the intense aroma of cooking greens and garlic. Papa Andrea attributed his long life to the habitual consumption of these vegetables and their cooking liquid.

I have chosen escarole as a model, but this method will work with any deep green vegetable from broccoli to kale. The only thing that varies is cooking time.

FOR FOUR SERVINGS

1 head escarole	sea salt
2 cloves garlic, chopped coarse	black pepper
¼ cup extra virgin olive oil	1 lemon, quartered

Cut off the stem end of the escarole. Soak the leaves in the sink filled with cold water. Meanwhile, chop the garlic.

Make sure that the leaves are free of dirt and place them in a pot with the garlic, salt, olive oil, and about ½ cup of water. Cook covered at medium heat for 15 minutes or until tender. Check it from time to time for sticking and add more water if necessary.

Serve it in bowls with lemon and black pepper to taste. Accompany it with good bread to dip in the liquid.

I CUCUZZEDDI
(Zucchini)

The lovely simplicity of boiled zucchini with hard ricotta (ricotta salata) grated on top is a good complement to a more complex meat or fish course.

FOR SIX SERVINGS

8 medium-sized zucchini
⅓ cup extra virgin olive oil
sea salt

black pepper
ricotta salata, coarse-grated
to sprinkle on top

Peel the zucchini. Cut them in half lengthwise and cross-cut them into pieces about ¼-inch thick. Place them in a pot with the olive oil and enough water to barely cover them. Salt. Cook covered at medium heat for about 10 minutes or until tender. Serve in little bowls with plenty of the liquid and the grated cheese sprinkled on top. Eat the *cucuzzeddi* with bread dipped in the liquid.

CARDUNA FRIUTA
(Fried Cardoons)

Carduna, also called in Italian *cardi* or *cardone*, is a stalklike vegetable with the texture of celery and the flavor of artichoke. It is always part of a Christmas Eve feast and is served fried.

To cook carduna, first peel off the strings and cut the stalks in 1-inch lengths. Blanch them in boiling water acidulated with lemon juice for five minutes. Drain them and, when cooled, pat them dry.

Pass the pieces through beaten egg and dust with flour. Panfry them in extra virgin olive oil until a rich, golden brown. Drain on brown paper and serve with salt.

FUNCI CHINI

(Stuffed Mushrooms)

FOR FOUR PERSONS

9 mushrooms, 2½ to 3 inches
   in diameter
¾ cup bread crumbs
½ cup locatelli or imported
   pecorino cheese, grated
3 sprigs Italian parsley,
   chopped fine

6 tablespoons olive oil
1 clove garlic, chopped fine
2 tablespoons marsala
sea salt
black pepper

Remove the stems from the mushrooms and clean both parts with a mushroom brush using cold water. Do not soak the mushrooms. Dry them thoroughly. If the bottom end of the stem is fibrous, cut it away and then chop the remaining stems.

Heat 2 tablespoons of the olive oil in a skillet on high heat until it is nearly smoking. Add the chopped mushroom stems, salt, and cook for a few minutes until the liquid they give off starts to evaporate. Add the marsala and continue to cook until the alcohol has evaporated. Remove the pan from the heat and add the bread crumbs. Mix thoroughly and turn them into a bowl to cool.

When cooled, add the grated cheese, parsley, and garlic.

Stuff the mushrooms with this mixture and place them in an oven pan greased with some of the olive oil. Drizzle the remaining olive oil on top. Bake at 350° to 400° for about 45 minutes.

CIPPUDDI CA MARSALA

(Onions Marsala)

1 large onion for each person
extra virgin olive oil
6 whole cloves for each onion

sea salt
coarse ground pepper
dry marsala

Carefully peel the onions. Stick six cloves in each onion, putting one on the bottom. Place them in a baking dish. Drizzle them with olive oil. Salt. Bake covered at 375° for 30 minutes.

Uncover, shower with marsala, and continue to cook for another 10 to 15 minutes until the onions are tender. Transfer to a warmed serving bowl, cover with the pan juices, and sprinkle with coarse ground black pepper.

CACUOCCIULI CHINI
(Stuffed Artichokes)

Select artichokes that are large, rounded, and closed, with long stems, rather than ones that are spiky and open. The latter condition means that they have begun to go to seed and will be dry and tough. Cook one artichoke for each serving.

THE STUFFING FOR EACH ARTICHOKE

½ cup toasted bread crumbs

¼ cup locatelli or imported
   pecorino cheese, grated

½ clove garlic, chopped very fine

ADDITIONAL INGREDIENTS

lemon

extra virgin olive oil

water

Cut off 1 to 1½ inches from the top of each artichoke straight across. Snap off straggling leaves from the stem and trim the points of the remaining leaves with scissors. Holding the artichoke with both hands, gently spread it open with your thumbs. Using a spoon, remove the purple spiny leaves from the center and scrape out the cottony choke. Better to lose a couple of tender leaves than to come upon the choke while eating. Rinse each artichoke under running water and shake dry.

Select a heavy pot with a lid in which the artichokes will stand up and fit tightly together. Trim the stems so that they stand nearly to the top of the pot. Try a test placement before stuffing.

Place the stuffing in a large bowl. Working over the bowl, press and tap stuffing in each artichoke. Move from the outer leaves toward the center. It is not necessary to fill up the cavity where the choke was removed, but it should have some stuffing in it.

When all the artichokes are standing up in the pot, place the juice and rind of one lemon for every four artichokes in the bottom of the pot. Be careful not to get any lemon juice on top of the artichokes. Pour water into the pot, again avoiding the tops so that the stems are standing in water to ½ inch below the bottoms of the artichokes. Drizzle extra virgin olive oil on the top of each artichoke.

Cover and cook at low heat for 50 minutes to one hour. Check from time to time to make sure all the water hasn't evaporated. Serve hot.

RISU PILAU
(Rice Pilaf)

This method of cooking rice is originally Turkish. It is a very convenient method, as it requires no attention.

Choose a lidded pot that can later go into the oven and liberally grease it with extra virgin olive oil. Place it on the stove at medium heat. When the oil is warm, add the rice. Turn the rice in the oil for a couple of minutes. Make sure it doesn't brown.

When the rice is warmed and well coated, pour in a volume of boiling water equal to two times the volume of the rice. Salt. When the water returns to the boil, cover and place in a preheated 350° oven for exactly 18 minutes.

To this basic recipe one can use a variety of condiments or substitute the water with broth. To create a decidedly Levantine flavor, add a little orange peel, slivered almonds, and black pepper to the rice before putting it in the oven.

RISU 'NINSALATA
(Rice Salad)

As part of a buffet, or on a summer's night, this rice salad offers a colorful alternative to a hot accompaniment.

FOR SIX SERVINGS

1 pound (about 2 cups) arborio rice
½ cup shelled peas
2 tablespoons capers, rinsed
1 small bell pepper,
   cut in narrow strips
¾ cup chopped black olives
¼ cup sultanas or white raisins,
   plumped in white wine or water

⅓ cup slivered almonds
½ cup extra virgin olive oil
¼ cup lemon juice
sea salt
black pepper

Cook the rice in a large pot of lightly salted boiling water. While it is cooking, drop the peas in a small pot of boiling water for five minutes and drain them.

When the rice is cooked, drain it and mix it with the capers, pepper, olives, raisins, and almonds.

Whisk the lemon juice and olive oil together with a little salt and dress the rice salad with it.

Add the peas last so they do not crush. Serve at room temperature.

CIPPUDEDDI AURUDUCI

(Sweet and Sour Onions)

FOR SIX SERVINGS

1¼ pounds small boiling onions
(about 30 onions)
1 tablespoon butter
1 tablespoon extra virgin olive oil

3 tablespoons white wine vinegar
4 tablespoons honey
coarse ground black pepper

Blanch the onions. That is to say, cook them in boiling water for about 2 minutes and drain. When they are cool enough to handle, remove the skin.

In a skillet large enough to accommodate all the onions in one layer, melt the butter and olive oil at low heat. Turn the onions in the fat until they are well covered. Sprinkle the vinegar over the onions slowly. Let it cook and evaporate for a few minutes.

Add the honey, again turning the onions in it. Let it cook at a gentle flame until the sauce is creamy and caramel colored. Transfer to a serving platter and add the coarse ground black pepper.

Serve at room temperature or slightly chilled. These onions are wonderful with fish or meats.

❧

PUMADAMURI VERDI 'NINSALATA

(Green Tomato Salad)

In the Madonie Mountains the growing season is short. Tomatoes that have had enough time to turn red are prized and used for fresh tomato sauce or canned for use in sauce during winter. Only the green ones, which will not have enough time to turn red before the frost, are eaten in salad.

To prepare this salad, choose green Roma or plum tomatoes. Those that are half red, half green may also be used. Cut them in quarters or sixths, depending on their size. Arrange them on a serving platter. Salt and sprinkle liberally with dried oregano. Drizzle extra virgin olive oil and grind black pepper on top.

The tomatoes are acidic enough so that vinegar or lemon juice is not warranted.

INSALATA 'I PATATI
(*Potato Salad*)

Peel and cut white or red potatoes. Boil in lightly salted water until cooked. Drain. While still hot, toss with a generous amount of extra virgin olive oil, a few chopped anchovies, and several thin slices of red onion. Sprinkle capers and black pepper on top.

It is best not to refrigerate this potato salad before serving, as the oil will coagulate and the potatoes will turn dry and mealy. Serve it at room temperature.

ARANCI E FINUCCHI 'NINSALATA
(*Orange and Fennel Salad*)

The unlikely combination of oranges and fennel with garlic and salt creates a wonderful flavor. *Aranci e finucchi 'ninsalata* can be eaten as an antipasto or as an accompaniment to a simple second course of either meat or fish or as a salad course after the second course. Wherever it appears in the meal, however, it must always be eaten with bread.

For this salad choose oranges that are the most bitter available. If bitter oranges are not in season, bitter tangerines can be a good substitute.

FOR SIX SERVINGS

4 large oranges
1 medium-sized fennel bulb
2 tablespoons fennel leaves,
  chopped

2 cloves garlic, chopped
4 tablespoons extra virgin olive oil
sea salt

Cut the oranges in quarters or sixths. Working over the serving bowl to catch the juice, peel and remove the seeds from each section.

Cut the fennel from the root end into thin slices. Remove and discard the core, and add these slices to the orange slices.

Add the garlic, salt, and toss. Add the olive oil and toss again. Sprinkle with chopped fennel leaves. Serve slightly chilled.

INSALATA 'I LINTICCHI
(Lentil Salad)

Sicilians believe that every lentil eaten on New Year's Eve will produce an equal number of gold coins in the coming year. Not to eat any lentils on New Year's Eve will produce unspeakable bad luck for the next twelve months, so they say.

FOR SIX SERVINGS

1 cup lentils	4 sprigs mint, chopped
⅓ cup extra virgin olive oil	2 tablespoons white wine vinegar
1 bunch scallions,	sea salt
chopped very fine	black pepper

Place the lentils in a pot and cover with cold water. Bring slowly to a boil, then turn down the heat and simmer for about 15 minutes until the lentils are cooked but remain firm and intact.

Drain the lentils thoroughly and toss immediately with the olive oil, salt, scallions, mint, and black pepper. Serve at room temperature.

⚜

INSALATA MISTA
(Mixed Green Salad)

As Papa Andrea taught me, making a good salad is more art than science. It is not, however, a difficult art to master.

Essential are a good mix of sweet and bitter ingredients, such as butter lettuce, radicchio, watercress, fennel, endive, and red onion. Be sure the lettuce is washed and well dried. Tear it into pieces; never cut it.

Place the ingredients in a salad bowl, the bigger, the better. Add plenty of sea salt and toss the mixture. The salt will open the lettuce to receive the vinegar, which is added next. Sprinkle enough good wine vinegar to have its aroma rise from the bowl, but not be overpowering. Toss the salad for a second time.

Now add the best quality extra virgin olive oil available. The rule of thumb is three times as much oil as vinegar. Toss the salad again. Add coarse ground black pepper and serve.

The result should be neither vinegary nor oily, and the taste of the ingredients should be enhanced by the dressing, not overpowered by it.

A mixed green salad is a great accompaniment to fried foods or as its own course served after the second.

I Cosi Duci

(Sweets)

Some believe that European pastry-making began in Sicily, it being the first stop for sugar from North Africa. For centuries, pastries were made by nuns for saint's days and special occasions. Unfortunately, these "convents of the sweet tooth" barely exist today.

I am told that my great-grandfather, Cologero Vilardi, was an extraordinary pastry chef. He died in 1907. As the story goes, shortly after his death, a close friend of the family borrowed his recipe book and never returned it, claiming it was lost. The family knew this to be untrue because this person would supply the family with extraordinary pastries and cookies at every holiday, claiming their creation for herself. Over the years, some of these recipes were returned to my mother and in turn, I have included them in this book.

The story of my great-grandfather goes on to say that he belonged to a secret mystical organization named "La Società di Santa Brigida." Its members, through certain prayers and observances, would recognize the day on which they were to die. One morning, when he was forty-nine and living in New York, he went to his pastry shop and gave away all the sweets to his customers. He went home for lunch, after which he gave his daughter, my grandmother, a bottle of cherry liqueur he had recently made, telling her to save it to drink on a special occasion. Something frightened her about this request. He assured her that everything was all right, and said he was going to bed to take a nap. A short while later, he was roused by a door-to-door salesman selling rag rugs. He bought one for my grandmother and then, assuring her a second time, returned to his nap. That afternoon, he died peacefully in his sleep. The family has not yet found an occasion special enough on which to drink the liqueur.

FRAGULI SUTTU SPIRITU
(Strawberries Soaked in Sweet Vermouth)

Whenever Papa Andrea bought strawberries, he always sliced them, sugared them, and soaked them in sweet vermouth overnight before we could eat them. As a boy, the wait to eat these rubies seemed endless to me. I would ask my grandfather if they were ready, and he would say, "No, my boy, they're not cooked yet."

When I was twenty years old and in acting school, I saw a fellow student eating strawberries out of the box. I told him with great assurance, "Those must taste terrible raw!" I have since learned that strawberries are quite delicious on their own. I do, however, think it at the very least barbaric to eat them "raw"!

Select very red and firm strawberries. To prepare them for soaking, clean them, hull them, and slice them in half. Shake a liberal amount of powdered sugar over them and stir until it is all dissolved. Pour enough sweet vermouth over the strawberries to cover them. Cover the bowl and let them soak overnight in the refrigerator.

These strawberries may be served on their own or with whipped cream, ice cream, or anything else you find appropriate.

BIANCUMANCIARI
(Cornstarch Pudding)

The simplicity of *biancumanciari,* a pudding, delicately flavored with lemon and cinnamon, makes it an excellent light dessert.

FOR EIGHT SERVINGS

2 quarts milk	peel of one lemon,
2 cups sugar	cut in wide strips
½ cup cornstarch	ground cinnamon

Set out eight china cups or small bowls with a piece of lemon peel in each one.

Dissolve the cornstarch in ½ cup of milk. Use a whisk to make certain it is smooth with no lumps. Place it, together with the rest of the milk, sugar, and two pieces of lemon peel, in a saucepan. Cook over low heat, stirring constantly with a wooden spoon to make sure the milk doesn't stick, burn, or boil. As it cooks, the pudding will begin to form in lumps. Continue cooking and stirring until it is smooth and thick. Pour immediately into the cups.

When cooled, chill the pudding uncovered in the refrigerator for three hours. Serve with a light dusting of ground cinnamon.

BUDINU 'I RISU
(Rice Pudding)

Everyone's grandmother has a rice pudding recipe. *Budinu 'i risu* is from mine.

FOR EIGHT SERVINGS

1 cup arborio rice	4 egg yolks
2 quarts +1 cup milk	1 tablespoon vanilla
1 cup sugar	ground cinnamon
4 tablespoons cornstarch	

Cook the rice until it is two minutes underdone, in very lightly salted boiling water. Drain it thoroughly.

Set out eight china coffee cups or small bowls.

Dissolve the cornstarch in one cup of milk. Use a whisk to make certain there are no lumps.

In a separate bowl, beat the egg yolks and sugar together until the mixture is pale yellow and forms ribbons. Whisk in the vanilla and cornstarch mixture.

Pour the two quarts of milk into the large saucepan and scald it over low heat; that is to say, bring it to 185° or until small bubbles form around the edge of the pot. Stir it with a wooden spoon so the milk doesn't stick, burn, or boil.

Now add the rice. If the rice has stuck together, break it up with a wooden spoon. When the rice is warm, add the egg yolk mixture and stir constantly until the pudding is thick and smooth.

Pour it into the coffee cups and when it is cooled, chill it in the refrigerator uncovered, for three hours. Serve with plenty of ground cinnamon on top.

L'OVA 'SBATUTA
(Zabaglione)

Papa Andrea enjoyed serving *l'ova 'sbatuta*, more as a restorative than a dessert. He prepared it every morning for my grandmother, who was anemic and frail. I suspect, however, that it has no medicinal value whatsoever, but it was pleasing to wake up to its lovely aroma.

The technique for success here is not difficult, but may require a little practice. Cook l'ova 'sbatuta in a double boiler arranged so that the water does not touch the upper bowl, only its steam. As always with egg yolk preparations, it works best if the upper bowl is made of copper.

For each person, use 2 egg yolks, 2 teaspoons sugar, 4 tablespoons sweet marsala, and a little finely chopped orange zest. Whisk the egg yolks and sugar together until they are pale yellow and frothy. Whisk in the marsala and orange zest. Place the mixture in the upper bowl of the double boiler and cook. Whisk constantly until it is the consistency of thick paint. Do not let it boil. Boiling will cause it to collapse. Serve immediately in warmed dessert cups.

CANNOLA
(Cannoli)

Cannola is so typically Sicilian that in other parts of Italy, this delicious dessert is often called *Cannoli alla Siciliana*. The recipe for the shells given here is from my great-grandfather Cologero Vilardi. The shells are rolled out, wrapped around a metal form, then deep-fried in a light oil. The metal forms are readily available in gourmet cookware shops. They are tubes, usually made of tin, about six inches long and one inch in diameter.

Cannola are stuffed with a ricotta cream. Because the ricotta generally available in America is of poor quality, I have included a recipe for making it. It is quite simple, as you will see, but the superior results give the illusion of much greater effort.

CANNOLA SHELLS

ABOUT 24 SHELLS

1³⁄₄ cups flour	1 egg, slightly beaten
2 tablespoons powdered sugar	¹⁄₄ cup dry white wine
¹⁄₄ teaspoon cinnamon	1 egg white, beaten, for sealing
¹⁄₂ generous teaspoon	2 quarts light oil, such as safflower,
cocoa powder	sunflower, canola, or sesame,
pinch salt	for frying
2 tablespoons firm butter	

Sift together, two times, the flour, sugar, cinnamon, cocoa powder, and pinch of salt. Cut in the butter, then the beaten egg. Add the white wine slowly, until a ball is formed. Knead the dough just enough to achieve an elastic consistency. Excessive kneading will cause the pastry to become tough. Place the dough on a floured cloth and let it rest for 15 minutes.

Meanwhile, begin to heat the oil to 350° in a 3¹⁄₂-quart pot.

After the dough has rested, take about a quarter of it, leaving the rest covered, and roll it with a lightweight rolling pin to ¹⁄₁₆-inch thickness. Use a cookie cutter or a small bowl to cut the dough in circles 4 inches in diameter. Using the rolling pin, shape these circles into ovals. Wrap the oval, the narrow way, securely around the form. Where it overlaps in the center, seal it with beaten egg white. Be certain not to "glue" the dough to the form with the egg white. Flare the edges to create that lovely cannola shape.

Drop several of the cannola into the heated oil. Fry for a couple of minutes until they are a rich brown color. Remove from the pot and place on brown paper to absorb the grease. When cool enough to handle, remove each form with a slight twist.

Cannola shells may be made the day before and left uncovered in a dry place. They must not be filled until immediately before serving, as the shells will become soft and rubbery from the moisture of the ricotta cream.

RICOTTA

THIS RECIPE YIELDS ABOUT TWO POUNDS OF CHEESE,

ENOUGH FOR ONE RECIPE OF CANNOLA SHELLS.

(1)
(½)
     1½ gallons milk

     ¾ cup white distilled vinegar

        to 5 percent (This is common

        supermarket white vinegar.)

     sea salt

Heat the milk evenly, stirring occasionally, to 185°; that is to say, scald it. When little bubbles form around the edge of the pot, remove the pot from the heat and add the vinegar. Stir well. You will notice that the milk has curdled and the ricotta has begun to form. Cover the pot with cheesecloth and let it stand, unrefrigerated, overnight.

Next morning, drain the cheese. For this purpose, an unglazed basket is traditionally used but a plastic basket or colander will also work. If you are using a basket, make sure it is clean by rinsing it under hot water. Do not use soap. Line your drainer with two layers of cheesecloth, cut generously enough to rise above the sides.

Pour in the contents of the pot and allow it to drain freely for about half an hour. Then make a package out of the cheesecloth; twist and squeeze it until the liquid begins to run milky. Turn the cheese out into a bowl, and add about ¼ teaspoon of salt.

If for some reason you cannot make homemade ricotta, prepare 2½ pounds of the store-bought variety in the following manner:

Heat it in a nonreactive frying pan slowly, until the cheese expels its liquid, then drain it through cheesecloth. This will work, but I repeat, it is inferior to the homemade variety.

RICOTTA CREAM

2 pounds ricotta	½ cup chocolate chips
1½-2 cups powdered sugar, sifted	¼ cup candied citron, orange
1 tablespoon vanilla	or lemon, chopped
2 tablespoons orange liqueur	

Pass the ricotta through a large-holed screen of a food mill in order to break up the curds. Mix in the sugar by hand with a wooden spoon. Do not use a mixing machine, which will destroy the curds. Mix in the vanilla and the liqueur, and then fold in the citron. Refrigerate. Be sure the mixture is completely cooled before folding in the chocolate chips.

Immediately before serving, stuff the cannola shells using a pastry bag, a spoon, or a spatula. Stuff them from one end, and then the other. Decorate each one with candied orange peel or candied cherries, or both. Dust with powdered sugar and serve.

Cannola are traditionally eaten with the fingers. Drago, a fine Sicilian-Italian restaurant in Los Angeles, has devised a most elegant way of serving cannola which, at the same time, puts guests at ease about picking it up with their fingers. They make a tracing by placing a fork on a large plate, lightly dusting that area of the plate with cocoa powder, then removing the fork. Next to this tracing they place the cannola.

ACCEDDU CU L'OVA
(Easter Cakes)

Acceddu cu l'ova is Sicilian for "bird with an egg." The shapes of these cookies can be quite elaborate, but my favorite is suggestive of bird wings or rabbit ears. These cakes, with the hard-cooked egg in the center, are a great breakfast treat throughout the Easter season. This recipe is from my great-grandfater Cologero.

FOR ONE DOZEN CAKES

1 dozen brown or colored medium eggs, raw	½ cup milk
	4 cups flour
1 cup sugar	3 teaspoons baking powder
¾ cup vegetable shortening	pinch salt
1 teaspoon vanilla	1 egg white, beaten
4 eggs	nonpareils

Cream the sugar and shortening. Add the vanilla and eggs. Mix together very thoroughly. Sift together the flour, baking powder, and a pinch of salt. Add it to the sugar mixture and then add the milk. Mix it together just enough to form the dough. This dough will be very soft, but if it is too sticky, add more flour; too dry, add more milk. Cover and let it rest for 10 minutes.

Meanwhile, cover a cookie sheet with kitchen parchment.

Divide the dough into twelve equal parts. Using the palms of your hands, roll each piece into a cigar shape, about 12 inches long. Cut off two 1-inch pieces from each cigar.

Working on the parchment, form each cigar into a U shape. Place the egg horizontally into the curve of the U. Roll the little pieces and crisscross them over the egg. Slightly turn out the top of the U. Using the point of a sharp knife or a dough scraper, form little hash marks along the outer edges of the U to make a decorative pattern. Place the cakes about 2 inches apart on the sheet.

When the cookie sheet is full, brush each one with slightly beaten egg whites and sprinkle with nonpareils. Bake for about 20 minutes, or until golden brown, in the center of a preheated 400° oven. The egg, of course, hard cooks in the oven.

CUCIADDATU
(*Christmas Pastry*)

Cuciaddatu is another of the known authentic recipes from my great-grandfather Cologero Vilardi. The poor people of the region prepare this Christmas pastry with dried figs; the rich, with raisins. In these Sicilian mountains fig trees are plentiful and one can always find figs to dry. But to have raisins, one must own a vineyard.

Traditionally, this pastry is formed in the shape of a log, but Papa Andrea often formed individual turnovers.

The women of Polizzi Generosa, a small mountain city, still gather in small groups during the Christmas season to bake their cuciaddatu in wood-burning ovens.

FOR TWO LOGS OR ABOUT FIVE DOZEN TURNOVERS

FOR THE PASTRY

2 pounds flour

1 cup confectioners' sugar

3 pinches salt

1 pound (2 cups) vegetable
shortening

8 whole eggs

+2 yolks, beaten together

3 tablespoons cognac

FOR THE FILLING

½ pound blanched almonds	2 teaspoons unsweetened
½ pound filberts or hazelnuts	cocoa powder
½ cup (3 ounces) pine nuts	2 tablespoons cognac
1 pound +2 ounces raisins	¼ cup water
¾ cup honey	2 beaten egg whites
¼ cup sugar	nonpareils
2 teaspoons cinnamon	

Toast the filberts in a hot oven for about five minutes. Be sure they do not burn. When they are cool enough to handle, rub them together to remove as much of the inner shell as possible. Chop together the filberts, almonds, and raisins.

Heat the honey, sugar, cinnamon, cocoa, cognac, and water together, bringing the mixture slowly to a boil. Let it boil for five minutes. Turn in the chopped nuts and raisins, and the whole pine nuts. When they are well coated, remove the pot from the heat and allow it to cool.

Meanwhile, prepare the dough. Sift together the flour, sugar, and three pinches of salt. Cut in the shortening, then cut in the beaten eggs and egg yolks. Mix in the cognac, and knead just until the dough is elastic. Form it into a ball, lightly dust it, cover it in a cloth, and let it rest for 15 minutes.

If you are preparing logs, divide the dough in half and roll it into two rectangles, ¼-inch thick. Place half the filling on each, form it into a log shape, seal the seam very well, close the ends, and place seam-side-down onto a cookie sheet. Brush with egg white and decorate with nonpareils. Bake in a 350° oven for one hour or until a pale golden color. When the logs are completely cooled, wrap them in plastic wrap to ensure freshness.

If you are making turnovers, roll out the dough, fairly thin, about ¹⁄₁₆ inch. Cut out 4-inch circles. Place a small mound of the nut-and-raisin mixture on half of the circle, about ¼ inch in from the edge. Brush the edge with beaten egg white. Fold over the other half, and pinch the seam together to form a tight seal. Place it on a cookie sheet.

When the cookie sheet is filled, brush the top of each turnover with egg white and decorate with nonpareils. Bake in a preheated 350° oven for about 20 minutes, or until barely golden on top.

When they are completely cooled, store them in a closed cookie tin to ensure freshness.

SFINCI AMMILATI
(Puffs With Honey)

In my family, we ate *sfinci* after midnight on New Year's Eve. They are made of deep-fried choux pastry soaked in honey and cinnamon. They are eaten warm. Sfinici must have been one of Cologero Vilardi's favorite desserts. He held one on the end of a fork in a photo that is reprinted in this book.

FOR ABOUT 24 SFINCI

1 cup (2 sticks) unsalted butter

2 cups water

2 cups flour, sifted

8 eggs

2 quarts light oil, such as safflower,
     sunflower, canola, or sesame,
     for frying

³/₄ cup honey

¹/₄ cup water

¹/₂ teaspoon cinnamon

confectioners' sugar

Melt the butter in the water in a saucepan. When it comes to a boil, stir in the sifted flour. Continue stirring and cooking until the mixture is smooth and leaves the sides of the pan. Remove from heat and turn into a bowl. Add the eggs one at a time, mixing thoroughly before adding another. Let the batter cool.

Meanwhile, place the honey, water, and cinnamon in a small saucepan on the stove, but do not heat it yet.

Pour the oil in a 3¹/₂-quart pot and heat it until it is very hot, 375°. When the oil is ready, take a mounded soupspoon of the batter, and using a second soupspoon, scrape it off and drop it into the oil. Fry until golden brown and hollow inside, and then remove it from the oil with a slotted spoon. Roll it on brown paper to absorb the grease. Place it on a warmed serving platter.

When the sfinci are nearly all cooked, heat the honey and cinnamon. When the liquid comes to a boil, turn down the heat and keep it warm until all of the sfinci are cooked and arranged on the platter. Pour the honey over them, dust with powdered sugar, and serve immediately.

SFINCI 'I SAN GIUSEPPI
(Filled Puffs)

For St. Joseph's Feast Day, which is March 19, a filled version of sfinci are made. Fry the sfinci until they are darker in color than previously stated. This is done so that there is no chance of collapse after they are cooled.

Just before serving, make a slit in the top of each sfinci and fill it to overflowing with the same ricotta cream as that for cannola. Decorate with candied peel and dust with powdered sugar.

For 24 sfinci 'i San Giuseppi, you will need one and one-half times the recipe for ricotta cream.

⚜

MINNI 'I VIRGINI
(Virgins' Breasts)

According to Butler in *The Lives of the Saints*, St. Agatha, who lived in the third century in Sicily, was a beautiful girl from a rich and illustrious family and consecrated to God at an early age. She became the obsession of a Roman consul, who believed he could easily despoil her virtue and steal her estates by using the emperor's edict against Christians. When his wicked designs failed, he had her sent to a brothel to wear down her resistance. When he was told of her continued constancy, he ordered her to be stretched on the rack. Seeing her suffer all this with cheerfulness so enraged him that he ordered her tortured and her breasts to be cut off. She was then placed in a dungeon and left to die. A miracle, however, occurred and she was completely restored. This further enraged the consul, who had her rolled naked over live coals mixed with potsherds, and that, in fact, caused her martyrdom.

During the era of the great monasteries in Sicily, nuns began a tradition of making mounded almond pastries filled with candied cucuzza or biancumanciari to celebrate St. Agatha's Feast Day, February 5.

FOR ONE DOZEN PASTRIES

FOR THE BIANCUMANCIARI FILLING

2 1/2 cups milk	piece of lemon peel
1/2 cup sugar	1/2 cup chocolate chips
6 tablespoons cornstarch	8 green candied cherries, chopped fine

2 cups flour	2 eggs, beaten
1 cup almond meal	1 teaspoon cognac
⅓ cup confectioners' sugar	1 tablespoon milk
¾ cup vegetable shortening	6 red candied cherries, cut in half

Make a thick biancumanciari using the ingredients listed here and the method explained earlier in this chapter. When it is ready, turn it into a bowl and stir it from time to time until it is cooled. Remove the lemon peel and add chopped candied green cherries. Refrigerate it, uncovered, for two hours. When it is chilled, fold in the chocolate chips.

Sift together the flour, almond meal, sugar, and a pinch of salt. Cut in the shortening and then the beaten eggs. Add the cognac and milk. Knead it until it is elastic. Form it into a ball, cover, and refrigerate for one and a half hours.

Roll out the dough to ⅛-inch thickness on a lightly floured work surface. This dough tends to be crumbly. Roll it in small quantities, pushing it down with your hand and then completing the task with a rolling pin. Cut out 12 circles 4 inches in diameter and 12 circles 2½ inches in diameter. Place a small mound of biancumanciari, about 1 inch high, in the center of the larger circle ¾ of an inch in from the edge. Brush the edge with egg white. Using a spatula, lift it into the palm of your cupped hand. Place the small circle on top and join the two pieces of dough together. Maintain a mounded shape and place it with the small circle down on a cookie sheet. Place one half of a red candied cherry on top.

When all the pastries are formed, bake in a preheated 375° oven for 15 minutes, or until a light golden color. Serve slightly chilled.

SFUAGGHIU
(*Polizzian Cheesecake*)

Sfuagghiu is the pastry specialty of Polizzi Generosa, the small city in Sicily from which my family came. It is known only by repute in neighboring towns, but its fame reaches as far as Palermo.

Part of the unique flavor and texture of this double-crusted cheesecake is produced by the meringue into which the cheese, flavored with sugar, cinnamon, cocoa, and candied fruits, is folded. Mostly, however, this uniqueness is due to the cheese, which is called *tuma* or, in the local dialect, *'a schuarata*. It is a fresh-pressed sheep's milk cheese, unsalted. Some Italian food stores here can acquire a cow's milk version on special order from their cheese suppliers. This unsalted tuma from cow's milk works very well; the recipe may be halved for smaller cakes.

FOR ONE 10-INCH DIAMETER BY 2 INCHES DEEP CHEESECAKE

FOR THE CRUST

4 cups flour	6 egg yolks, beaten
1 pinch sea salt	$\frac{1}{2}$ cup water
$\frac{3}{4}$ cup confectioners' sugar	confectioners' sugar in a shaker
1 cup vegetable shortening	

FOR THE FILLING

2 pounds tuma	$\frac{1}{2}$ teaspoon unsweetened
$1\frac{1}{2}$ cups sugar	cocoa powder
6 egg whites	$\frac{1}{2}$ teaspoon powdered cinnamon
$\frac{1}{8}$ teaspoon powdered eggshell	6 candied cherries, chopped fine
(see Pan 'i Spagna for method)	

Prepare and bake the cake the day before it is to be served. Let it stand uncovered and unrefrigerated in a cool place overnight.

Grate the cheese very fine. Because of its rubbery consistency, the cheese does not grate well on a standard box-type grater. Better results can be achieved in a food processor or by chopping it very fine with a sharp knife. When the cheese is grated, place it in a fine strainer lined with double cheesecloth over a bowl to drain.

Meanwhile, prepare the crust. Sift together the flour, confectioners' sugar, and a pinch of salt. Thoroughly cut in the shortening and then the egg yolks. Add the water until the dough is soft. Depending on weather conditions, you may need more or less water. Knead it just until it is elastic. Over-kneading will make the crust tough.

Form the dough into a ball, flour it, and cover it in a dishcloth. Let it rest for 10 minutes. If the weather is very hot, place it in the refrigerator to stiffen a bit. When the dough is ready, divide it into two balls, one $\frac{1}{4}$ larger than the other. Re-cover the smaller ball and roll the larger into a 15-inch circle about $\frac{1}{4}$-inch thick. Carefully line a 10-inch by 2-inch cheesecake pan with removable sides or bottom. Make sure there are no holes or thin spots in the crust.

Uncover the smaller ball and roll it into a 10-inch circle. Leave it on the work surface while preparing the filling. Preheat the oven to 375°.

In a clean, dry bowl, beat the egg whites and the powdered eggshell until they form high peaks.

At this point, begin to sprinkle in half the sugar while beating. Sprinkle the sugar slowly into the mixture to make certain the egg whites do not collapse. Refrigerate the meringue while preparing the cheese.

Squeeze the cheese in the cheesecloth of its excess liquid. In a dry bowl, mix it thoroughly with half of the sugar, the cinnamon, the cocoa, and the candied cherries.

Fold this meringue and the cheese together and turn it out into the pan. Gently tap it to remove air pockets. Gently and quickly put the top crust in place and seal the edges well. Bake at 350° for about an hour, until the crust turns a light golden color.

Turn off the heat and let the cake cool in the oven with the door ajar. A quick change in temperature may cause the filling to collapse. When the cake is cooled, turn it upside down onto a serving plate and remove the pan. Leave the cake unrefrigerated and in a cool place overnight.

Just before serving, cover the top and sides of the sfuagghiu with powdered sugar.

TORTA 'I RICOTTA
(Ricotta Pie)

FOR ONE 8 INCH IN DIAMETER BY 2-INCH DEEP PIE

THE CRUST

³/₄ cup flour

¹/₄ cup almond meal

2 tablespoons confectioners' sugar

pinch salt

¹/₄ cup shortening

1 egg, beaten

1 teaspoon cognac

THE FILLING

Half the recipe for the homemade ricotta listed in this book (see Cannola recipe) or the store-bought equivalent, prepared in the manner stated.

4 eggs, beaten

¹/₂ cup cream

1 cup sugar

1 teaspoon vanilla

¹/₂ teaspoon ground cinnamon

2 tablespoons currants, soaked in amaretto

1 tablespoon cognac

2 tablespoons pine nuts

8 candied cherries, chopped

THE TOPPING

1 pint strawberries,
    soaked in vermouth (Fraguli
    suttu Spiritu), as described
    in this chapter.

Sift together the flour, almond meal, sugar, and a pinch of salt. Cut in the shortening and then the beaten egg. Add the cognac and form the dough into a ball. Dust it with flour, cover it with a cloth, and let it rest for 10 minutes.

Roll it out evenly in a circle about 13 inches in diameter. Place the dough in an 8-inch-diameter springform pan, or one with a removable bottom. Gently press the dough into the corners. Form a lip around the top with the excess. Cover the dough with kitchen parchment weighted with pie weights or dried beans, and pre-bake the crust in a 400° oven for five minutes. The crust is pre-baked so it will not be soggy from the filling. It is weighted in this process so that it will not bubble up.

Pass the ricotta through the largest holed disk of a food mill to break up the curds. Mix it together thoroughly with all the other filling ingredients. Pour the mixture into the crust and bake at 300° for one and one-half hours, or until the top is golden brown and the center is dry when pierced with a toothpick. Cool the torta in the oven, with the heat turned off and the oven door ajar. A quick change in temperature may cause it to collapse.

When the torta is completely cooled, arrange the strawberries on top. Pour a small amount of their liquid on each serving.

༝

PAN 'I SPAGNA
(Sponge Cake)

Pan 'i Spagna, a basic sponge cake, is an ingredient in the assembly of many Sicilian desserts. Before I list the recipe, however, I would like to say a few words about two of the ingredients listed here: "00" flour and powdered eggshell. "00" flour is an Italian product difficult to find in the United States. It is lighter and finer than the flour that we are accustomed to using. All of the other recipes in this book call for all-purpose flour, but pan 'i spagna works best with "00" or a mixture of ³/₄ unbleached and ¹/₄ cake flour (e.g. Swans Down).

Powdered eggshell for many years has been the secret ingredient of chefs to keep stiffened egg whites from collapsing. To prepare an eggshell for this purpose, discard the inner lining, wash the shell with warm water, and let it dry thoroughly. Keep it in a small jar, and pulverize a small piece as needed. I have found that the shell of one egg is enough for several years' use.

FOR ONE 8-INCH-SQUARE X 2-INCH-DEEP PAN 'I SPAGNA

5 eggs, separated	$\frac{1}{8}$ teaspoon powdered eggshell
1$\frac{1}{2}$ cups sugar	1 cup "00" flour or
1 teaspoon vanilla or	$\frac{3}{4}$ cup white flour and
1 teaspoon lemon zest,	$\frac{1}{4}$ cup cake flour
chopped fine	

Preheat the oven to 375°. Grease and flour an 8-inch-square baking pan.

Beat the egg yolks and sugar together until they turn pale yellow and form ribbons. Add the vanilla or lemon zest. Beat in the flour a little at a time, only adding more when the previous addition has been thoroughly absorbed.

Begin to beat the egg whites (in a copper bowl, if possible) with a clean whisk. If any oil from the egg yolks touches the egg whites, they will not stiffen. When the whites begin to change color, add the eggshell. Continue beating until they are stiff, but not dry. Add a few tablespoons of the whites to the yolk mixture, and beat it in to loosen it. Fold the whites and the yolks together, turn into the pan, and bake in the center of the oven for 40 minutes. If you must open the oven door, make the opening as small, gentle, and as fast as possible, as a sudden noise or gush of cold air could cause the cake to collapse.

When it is done, turn it out upside down on a cooling rack.

SUPPA INGLISI
(Meringue Cream Pie)

The semi-freddo is a whole category of wonderful Sicilian desserts that are cold but not frozen. *Suppa inglisi,* "English soup," is the Sicilian interpretation of an English trifle. It is composed of Pan 'i Spagna soaked in rum, *crema pasticceria,* and meringue.

FOR 8 TO 12 SERVINGS

1 recipe Pan i' Spagna
Brown rum, for soaking the
    sponge cake.

FOR THE CREMA PASTICCERIA

6 egg yolks

³/₄ cup sugar

1 teaspoon vanilla

³/₄ cup "00" flour

4¹/₂ cups milk

1 tablespoon lemon zest, chopped fine

FOR THE MERINGUE

6 egg whites

1¹/₄ cups sugar

¹/₈ teaspoon powdered eggshell

powdered sugar

candied fruits for decoration

Prepare the pan 'i spagna, and while it is cooling, prepare the crema pasticceria. Scald the milk; that is, heat until small bubbles form around the edge at approximately 185°— do not boil. Remove from heat, cover, and let it stand for 10 minutes.

Meanwhile, beat together the egg yolks, sugar, vanilla, and lemon zest until it is pale yellow and forms ribbons. Slowly add the sifted flour to the mixture, beating until it is all absorbed. Continuing to beat the mixture, add the scalded milk until it is blended well into it.

Bring the mixture to a boil slowly, stirring constantly. Continue stirring and boiling until the flour taste is cooked away. Remove it from the heat and stir from time to time while cooling to prevent skin from forming on top.

Next, prepare the meringue. Beat the egg whites and powdered eggshell until they are very stiff and form high peaks. Continue beating and add the sugar by sprinkling it over the top and beating it into the stiffened egg whites. Care should be taken not to add the sugar too quickly, as it will cause the egg whites to collapse. Store the meringue in the refrigerator until it is ready to use.

Cut off two of the baked edges of the pan 'i spagna, discard, and cut the rest of the sponge in ¹/₂-inch thick slices.

Choose a 12-inch diameter, 2-inch deep, ovenproof pan (terra cotta is best) that will later be suitable for serving the suppa inglisi.

When the crema has reached room temperature, you can begin assembling. Place a few spoonfuls of crema in the bottom of the pan. Pour the rum into a shallow bowl. Pass a slice of the pan 'i spagna quickly through the rum so it doesn't absorb too much, and place it in the bottom of the pan. Continue this process until the pan is completely lined with one layer of pan 'i spagna. Cut pieces to fill in the spaces. Place the rest of the crema on top in an even layer. Cover with another layer of pan 'i spagna soaked in rum. Mound the meringue in an even layer on the top. Manipulate it with a spatula to form little peaks.

Dust the top with powdered sugar and decorate it with candied fruits. Bake it in the top portion of the oven, preheated to 250°, until the meringue is a light golden color. Let it cool, and then refrigerate overnight before serving.

BISCOTTI 'I FINUCCHI
(Fennel Seed Cookies)

These cookies, which are not very sweet, make an excellent accompaniment to ices and sorbets. As they get harder, they are great with morning coffee. This recipe is from my great-grandfather. I have reduced it from the original, which is four times the quantity of the one given here.

MAKES TWO DOZEN COOKIES

4 cups flour
1 teaspoon baking powder
pinch salt
¼ cup vegetable shortening
¼ cup sugar

2 eggs
¼ cup milk
¼ cup anisette or pernod
2 tablespoons fennel seeds

Sift together the flour, baking powder, and salt. In another bowl, cream the shortening and sugar. Add the eggs, milk, anisette, and fennel seeds. Mix very well. While mixing, add the flour a little at a time, until the dough forms a ball. Cover and let it rest for ten minutes to amalgamate.

Take a small piece of dough and roll it between your hands into a cylinder about 4 inches long and 1 inch in diameter. Place it on a cookie sheet and form it into an S shape. Place the next one about 1¼ inches away. When the sheet is full, bake at 375°, until golden brown. Cool on a rack.

CECILINI
(Sesame Seed Cookies)

Cecilini are very good with coffee or, in the summer, with lemon ice. In a closed container, the cookies keep a long time—if you can keep them! This recipe is also from my great-grandfather.

2½ cups flour
1 cup cornstarch
1 teaspoon baking powder
½ teaspoon salt
1½ cups vegetable shortening

1 cup sugar
3 eggs
1 teaspoon vanilla
milk, for coating the cookies
sesame seeds

Cream the sugar and shortening. Beat the eggs and vanilla, mix them well into the shortening and sugar.

Sift together the flour, cornstarch, baking powder, and salt two times. Add slowly to the wet ingredients until it is all absorbed. The result should be a soft dough. If it is too sticky, add more flour; too dry, add more milk. Form the dough into a ball, flour it, cover it with a cloth, and let it rest in the refrigerator for half an hour.

Take a piece of the dough and, using your hands, roll it against a floured work surface until it is about ¾-inch in diameter. Cut it in 3-inch lengths. Coat each length with milk and roll it in sesame seeds. Place on a cookie sheet. Bake in the center of the oven, preheated to 375°, until a light golden color.

⚓

BISCOTTI 'I PAN 'I SPAGNA
(*Anisette Toast*)

These cookies are also a good accompaniment to ices, gelato, or coffee at breakfast. The recipe is from my great-grandfather.

2 cups flour	½ cup vegetable shortening
2 teaspoons baking powder	4 eggs
pinch salt	⅓ cup anisette or pernod
1 cup sugar	

Preheat the oven to 350°. Sift together the flour, baking powder, and salt. In a different bowl, cream the sugar and shortening. Add the eggs, one at a time, and the anisette.

Meanwhile, grease and flour a 9-inch x 12-inch x 2-inch baking pan.

When the wet ingredients are mixed well together, add the dry ingredients. The batter will be heavy and require smoothing with a spatula to get it into the pan evenly. Bake for about 20 minutes, until golden brown on top, and dry inside when pierced with a toothpick.

Cut it on the diagonal in strips ¾-inch thick. Cut the longer strips in half. Place them flat on a wire rack, and return to the oven until toasted a golden brown on both sides.

When the cookies are cool, stack them crisscrossed on a small serving plate three or four across. Store them uncovered.

I COSI DUCI FRIDDI

(Frozen Desserts)

The origins of Sicilian frozen desserts go back to the ancients, who would mix snow from the mountains with fruit juice. Later the frozen confection we know as sorbet was devised by the Saracens. "Sarbat" was made by freezing jasmine flower water and sugar.

In the sixteenth century, Charles I of England had two Sicilian sorbet chefs. Legend has it that they were bound under pain of death not to divulge their secrets. In the seventeenth century, Francesco Procopio opened the first coffee-house in Paris. So successful was this Sicilian's frozen desserts that the Cafe Procope is still a Paris treasure.

Today, Sicilians remain devoted to their frozen desserts. In large cities these desserts are obtainable, it seems, every three feet. In addition to being an after-dinner sweet, they serve to refresh and restore one from the intense summer heat of the Mediterranean.

To make these desserts, an ice cream machine is essential. They are available in a wide range of styles and prices, from simple hand-cranked ones using ice and salt to freeze the dessert, to electric freezer-type ones with direct-drive motors. In choosing one, aside from what your purse permits and your personal style finds appropriate, it is very important to know the minimum amount it will produce rather than the maximum. It would be impossible, for example, to make a multi-flavored dessert for four people if your machine's minimum capacity is one quart.

There is no mystery to the art of making delicious and beautiful frozen desserts. These recipes are ones which I have experimented with over the years. I hope they will lead you to your own favorite flavors.

GRANITA E SORBETTU
(Ices and Sorbets)

These are composed of flavoring or fruit pulp, sugar, and water. *Granita* has less sugar than *sorbettu*. Simple syrup, which is water and sugar boiled together for five minutes, is usually the form in which the sugar is added. This does, however, create a slight caramel flavor, which is uncomplementary to some fruits. Therefore, in those cases sugar water, which is to say, just heating the water warm enough to melt the sugar and turn clear, is preferred. In other cases, confectioners' or granulated sugar is added directly to the pulp.

Always use the ripest fruits and the best water. If the water in your area is heavily chlorinated, I suggest the use of spring water instead. Do not store granita and sorbettu for longer than a few days, as they will lose their fresh-fruit flavor.

Granita and sorbettu served in pleated paper cups is a charming style, reminiscent of ice vendors not only on the streets of Sicily, but around the world.

❦

GRANITA 'I LIMUNI
(Lemon Ice)

FOR FOUR SERVINGS

4 to 5 lemons, depending on their sweetness

1¼ cups water
1 cup sugar

Heat the water and sugar together until the sugar dissolves and the liquid turns clear. Remove from the heat.

Juice the lemons. Add the sugar water slowly until the desired sweetness is reached. Chill thoroughly, uncovered in the refrigerator. Process in an ice cream machine.

GRANITA 'I MELUNI
(Melon Ice)

Choose a small, very sweet and ripe melon with orange, green, or yellow meat. Reduce the flesh of this melon to a very fine, almost liquid consistency. This can be done by passing it through various-sized disks of a food mill.

Shake confectioners' sugar into the pulp. This type of sugar is used because the cornstarch in confectioners' sugar will serve to slightly thicken the mixture. Start with ¼ cup, adding more to taste.

Add one tablespoon of grappa or vodka. This will prevent the ice from freezing rock hard. Refrigerate uncovered until thoroughly chilled. Pour it into an ice cream machine and process.

❧

GRANITA 'I ANGURIA
(Watermelon Ice)

Choose a small, round, seedless watermelon, very ripe and sweet. Prepare a sugar water mixture with 1½ cups sugar and 2½ cups water. Heat the mixture just warm enough to melt the sugar and turn clear. Then pour it into a bowl to cool.

Reduce the flesh of the melon to a very fine pulp by passing it through the various-sized disks of a food mill.

When the sugar water is at room temperature, mix enough of it into the watermelon pulp to achieve the desired sweetness. Mix in a pinch of ground ginger and 1 to 2 tablespoons vodka. Chill the mixture in the refrigerator for 3 hours. Pour it into an ice cream machine and process.

At the end of this process, stir in small chopped pieces of semisweet chocolate to imitate watermelon seeds.

GRANITA 'I CIUCCULATU
(Chocolate Ice)

FOR EIGHT SERVINGS

½ cup good quality, unsweetened
cocoa powder

1 pinch cinnamon

1 cup sugar

4 cups water

Make a simple syrup by boiling together the sugar and 2½ cups water for five minutes.

Meanwhile, combine the cocoa and a pinch of cinnamon, together with ½ cup water, in a saucepan. Cook at very low heat, stirring constantly until it is melted and smooth.

When the simple syrup is ready, mix it well with the chocolate. Transfer the mixture to a bowl and add 1 cup water. Do not refrigerate this mixture before processing, as it will cause the cocoa butter to coagulate. When it is at room temperature, process in an ice cream machine.

❧

GRANITA 'I CAFFE
(Coffee Ice)

This recipe for coffee ice is very strong in flavor and therefore high in caffeine. I recommend using decaffeinated espresso. Serve the ice in small quantities. A little heavy cream unwhipped is great on top. Served in a glass with the cream well mixed in, it is a most extraordinary iced coffee.

FOR FOUR TO SIX SERVINGS

¾ cup finely ground decaffeinated
espresso coffee

¼ cup sugar

3 cups water

Fill a 3½-quart saucepan ⅔ full with water. When it comes to a boil, turn it off.

Place the ground coffee and sugar in a 1-quart canning jar uncovered and place it in the pot of water.

Bring the 3 cups of water to a boil in a kettle, turn it off, wait 2 minutes, and pour it into the jar over the coffee and sugar. Stir the mixture.

Turn the heat on under the pot of water with the jar in it to very low and let the coffee gently infuse for 30 minutes. Turn off the heat. Leave the coffee to cool to room temperature in this arrangement.

When cooled strain this coffee through a very fine strainer. Let it chill in a refrigerator for a couple of hours. Place it in an ice cream machine and process.

❧

SORBETTU 'I FRAGULI
(Strawberry Sorbet)

FOR SIX SERVINGS

1 pint fresh strawberries	2 tablespoons sweet vermouth
1½ cups water	1 pinch cinnamon
1 cup sugar	

Heat the water and the sugar together until it is just warm enough to melt the sugar and have it turn clear. Remove from the heat.

Hull and puree the strawberries. Mix with the sugar water, vermouth, and cinnamon. Chill thoroughly, uncovered in the refrigerator. Process in an ice cream machine.

❧

SORBETTU 'I CLEMENTINA
(Tangerine Sorbet)

Clementines are a very sweet variety of seedless tangerines. They are difficult to find in this country, but any sweet tangerine at the height of the season will do.

The addition of the frothy egg whites gives the sorbet a creamy consistency.

FOR SIX SERVINGS

³/₄ cup freshly squeezed orange juice	The juice of 1 lemon
1 cup sugar	The zest of 1 tangerine, chopped fine
¼ cup water	2 tablespoons brown rum
The juice of 8 to 10 tangerines (approximately 3 cups)	2 egg whites

Place the orange juice, sugar, and water in a saucepan. Turn heat to medium and stir until the sugar melts. Bring slowly to a boil and continue boiling gently for five minutes. Pour it into a bowl to cool.

When it is room temperature, mix it slowly into the tangerine and lemon juices until the proper sweetness is achieved. You may not use all of it, depending upon the sweetness of the juice. Add the zest and the rum.

In a separate bowl, whisk the egg whites until frothy. Slowly whisk in the juice mixture.

Chill uncovered in the refrigerator for three hours. Process in an ice cream machine.

&

SORBETTU 'I KIWI
(Kiwi Sorbet)

FOR FOUR SERVINGS

6 ripe kiwis	1 cup sugar
1¼ cups water	2 tablespoons brown rum

Bring the combined water and sugar slowly to a boil and cook for five minutes.

Peel and puree the kiwis. When the simple syrup has cooled, add it to the puree along with the rum. Chill thoroughly, uncovered in the refrigerator. Process in an ice cream machine.

Spuma

(Frozen "Foam")

Spuma means "foam." These frothy frozen confections are composed of flavoring or fruit pulp and sugar, with the addition of whipped cream or meringue or both.

They are removed from the freezer to soften before serving. The result is so light and delicate that one seems to be eating foam.

⚜

SPUMA 'I RAGINA NIURA
(Black Grape Spuma)

FOR SIX SERVINGS

1³/₄ pounds black grapes	¹/₄ teaspoon vanilla
³/₄ cup sugar	1 cup whipping cream
³/₄ cup water	amaretto or maraschino
juice of ¹/₂ large lemon	for soaking

Wash and remove the stems from 1¹/₂ pounds of the grapes. Pass them through a food mill using the disk with holes small enough to prevent the seeds from passing through. It is fine, however, if some of the skins do pass. Refrigerate uncovered for at least two hours.

Heat the water and sugar together until the sugar melts and the liquid turns clear. Remove from heat immediately and when it is at room temperature, refrigerate for two hours also.

Meanwhile, marinate the remaining grapes in amaretto or maraschino.

When the grape pulp is cold, add enough cold sugar water to achieve the desired sweetness. Add vanilla and lemon juice.

Whip the cream until it swells but is not completely stiff. Add the grape mixture to it.

Now process the mixture in an ice cream machine. When it is ready, transfer it to six ribbed paper cups, 6 fluid ounces each, or deep custard tins lined with plastic wrap and holding the same volume. Level the top of each container. Cover well with plastic wrap and freeze until set.

Half an hour before serving, turn each portion into a traditional stemmed ice cream dish and decorate with the marinated grapes. Let it stand unrefrigerated to soften before serving.

*T*his type of molded dessert is called a *pezzu duru* or "hard piece." The recipe here serves as an introduction to a later section in this book which deals with the making of these beautiful and delicious desserts in greater detail.

✤

SPUMA 'I LAMPUNI

(Raspberry Spuma)

FOR FOUR SERVINGS

1 pint raspberries

³/₄ cup sugar

¹/₄ cup heavy cream

Reduce the raspberries to a pulp by passing them through the various-sized disks of a food mill. This will also serve to remove a good number of the seeds. Mix the sugar very thoroughly into the pulp.

In a different bowl, beat the cream until it begins to swell but is nowhere near whipped.

Whisk the raspberry mixture slowly into the cream. Process in an ice cream machine.

If made in advance, it gets very hard in the freezer. Allow it to soften before serving.

Gelatu
(Ice Cream)

There are two basic mixtures for Sicilian *gelatu*. One of these bases is called *crema rinsforsata*. It is a cornstarch pudding (Biancumanciari). This base produces a gelatu that is thin, frank, and very cold—similar to what we call ice milk.

The other base is called *crema 'i gelatu*, similar to *creme anglaise*. It produces an ice cream that is richer, thicker, and creamier, and is achieved not by a concentration of butterfat, as with American ice cream, but from egg yolks, giving it a surprising lightness.

Both are excellent and complement different flavors.

CREMA 'I GELATU
("Creme Anglaise" Based Ice Cream)

This recipe is given in numbered steps, as reference is made to them in other gelato recipes in this section.

With the addition of lemon zest, this base makes an excellent lemony ice cream.

FOR SIX TO EIGHT PERSONS

2 ¼ cups milk	½ cup +1 heaping tablespoon sugar
1 cup cream	1 tablespoon water
5 egg yolks	the zest of 1 lemon, chopped fine

1. Scald the milk and cream, which is to say, warm at medium heat until little bubbles form around the edge. Do not boil it.
2. Take it off the heat, cover it, and let it rest for 10 minutes.
3. Place the egg yolks in a bowl—copper, if possible; add the water, and beat them slowly, adding the sugar until it is pale yellow and forms ribbons.
4. Add the milk and cream slowly, beating it into the eggs and sugar.
5. Create a double boiler, again using the copper bowl if possible, in which the water in the bottom pot does not touch the top bowl. Pour the mixture into the top bowl.
6. Cook over medium heat, continuously whisking, for two minutes after the water beneath begins to boil. Do not boil the crema.
7. Remove from the heat, stir in the lemon zest. When it has cooled to room temperature, refrigerate uncovered for at least three hours.
8. Now process in an ice cream machine.

GELATU 'I FICU
(Fig Ice Cream)

Marinating the figs in a thick syrup perfumed with maraschino liqueur and vanilla brings out their exquisite flavor. Use only the ripest, sweetest black figs.

FOR SIX TO EIGHT SERVINGS

1 recipe Crema 'i Gelatu

10 very ripe and sweet black figs

2¼ cups sugar

1 cup water

¼ cup maraschino liqueur

1 tablespoon vanilla

Prepare the syrup the day before it is needed. To do so, heat the water and sugar slowly until it comes to a boil. Be sure to stir it, while the sugar melts, to prevent scorching. Continue to boil it gently for five minutes. Remove it from the heat and allow it to cool.

When it is at room temperature, stir in the vanilla and maraschino. Refrigerate overnight.

The next day prepare the Crema 'i Gelatu until it is to be processed. While it is chilling, prepare the figs.

Peel the figs. Place them whole in an open bowl in one layer. Pour the chilled syrup over them. Cover and let them marinate unrefrigerated for two hours. Turn them in the marinade from time to time.

After this time has elapsed, fish the figs out of the marinade. Slice and puree them in a food mill to a very fine paste. Mix in a couple of tablespoons of the Crema 'i Gelatu to loosen the paste, and then slowly mix in the rest of the crema until it is well blended together.

Now process in an ice cream machine.

GELATU 'I CIUCCULATU
(Chocolate Ice Cream)

FOR FOUR TO SIX SERVINGS

FOR THE *CREMA*

2 1/4 cups milk

1/4-inch vanilla bean

4 egg yolks

1/2 cup sugar

FOR THE CHOCOLATE FLAVORING

1/4 cup + 1 teaspoon good quality, unsweetened cocoa powder

1/2 cup water

1/4 cup sugar

1 teaspoon cognac

1 pinch cinnamon

Prepare the chocolate by placing the cocoa, sugar, and cinnamon in the top half of a double boiler. Turn on the heat and stir in the water slowly until the chocolate and sugar dissolve. Add the cognac. Continue cooking for about 10 minutes until the mixture thickens to the consistency of heavy cream. Remove it from the heat.

Proceed with steps 1 to 3 for Crema 'i Gelatu, using no cream and no water.

Add the chocolate. Continue with steps 4 to 8, discarding the vanilla bean and using no lemon zest.

GELATU 'I NUCCEDDI
(Hazelnut Ice Cream)

FOR FOUR TO SIX SERVINGS

1 recipe Crema 'i Gelatu,
  without the lemon zest
1/4 pound hazelnuts
  or filberts, shelled

1/3 cup confectioners' sugar
1/2 cup milk
1 teaspoon vanilla extract

Toast the hazelnuts in a hot oven for about five minutes. Be sure they do not burn. When they are cool enough to handle, rub them together to remove as much of the inner shell as possible. Chop the nuts.

Place the sugar in a small saucepan just large enough to later contain the nuts. Without adding any water, cook the sugar over a very gentle flame, stirring onstantly until it achieves a blonde color. Turn in the nuts and transfer the mixture into a mortar.

When the mixture is cooled, pound it. Slowly add the milk to form it into a very fine paste. Pass the mixture through a food mill, fitted with the disk with the medium-sized holes.

Now make the Crema 'i Gelatu from steps 1 through 8, but instead of lemon zest, add the nut paste and the vanilla.

GELATU 'I PISTACCHIU
(Pistachio Ice Cream)

FOR FOUR TO SIX SERVINGS

FOR THE PISTACHIO FLAVORING

1 cup pistachio nuts, raw, shelled, and unsalted	$\frac{1}{4}$ cup milk
	2 tablespoons sugar

FOR THE *CREMA*

2$\frac{1}{4}$ cups milk	$\frac{1}{2}$ cup sugar
$\frac{1}{4}$-inch vanilla bean	1 pinch sea salt
4 egg yolks	

Using a mortar and pestle, pound the pistachios and sugar into a fine paste, adding the milk when necessary to lubricate.

Proceed with steps 1 through 8 for Crema 'i Gelatu, using no cream and no water and adding the pistachio paste and a pinch of salt instead of the lemon zest in step 7.

❧

GELATU 'I CASTAGNE
(Chestnut Ice Cream)

Chestnuts are an excellent flavor to complement the other ice cream base, crema rinsforsata. Served with whipped cream and a bittersweet chocolate sauce, this dessert is truly sublime.

FOR FOUR TO SIX SERVINGS

2$\frac{1}{4}$ cups milk	1 recipe chocolate flavoring from
$\frac{1}{2}$-inch vanilla bean	Gelatu 'i Ciucculatu
2 tablespoons cornstarch	$\frac{1}{2}$ pint heavy cream
1 cup sugar	$\frac{1}{4}$ cup confectioners' sugar, sifted
1 pound chestnuts, prepared in the same manner as for Capuni Chini 'i Castagne or 10 ounces cooked chestnuts, canned or jarred	

When the fresh chestnuts are cooked, or the canned ones have been drained, reduce them to a puree.

Mix one-half cup of the milk with the cornstarch and whisk it together until it is smooth. In a heavy saucepan, place the remaining milk, sugar, vanilla bean, and cornstarch mixture. Cook at medium heat, stirring constantly with a wooden spoon to avoid sticking or scorching until the milk is at the boiling point. Do not allow it to boil, however. Remove it from the heat immediately.

Please note that the vanilla bean must be removed, so watch for it through the remaining steps.

When the mixture has cooled somewhat, mix it with the chestnut puree into a homogeneous mixture.

Pass the mixture through a food mill whose disk has the smallest holes—to ensure homogeneity.

When the mixture has cooled to room temperature, refrigerate uncovered for three hours. During this time, prepare the chocolate sauce. When it is room temperature, refrigerate it.

When the ice cream mixture is cold, process it in an ice cream machine.

Place the confectioners' sugar and heavy cream in a bowl. Whip it until it is very thick. Assemble the dessert just before serving.

I Pezzi Duri

(Molded Frozen Desserts)

The garish expression of the Baroque in Sicily extended itself quite naturally to the molding of frozen desserts into elaborate sculptural forms. These *pezzi duri,* "hard pieces," ranged from the familiar three-flavored brick to elaborate multi-flavored bombes. They are great fun to create and amusing to serve.

Just about any type of container can be used as a mold for a frozen dessert, as long as it can be put in the freezer, and the dessert can be gotten out. It is best to line larger molds with plastic wrap to ensure a good, quick release. Smaller molds, such as mini-tart tins, will release their jewels by placing them in a small amount of warm water, in the bottom of an open bowl.

When pezzi duri are molded in the fruit itself, they are served with the rind as the container. The rind, of course, is not lined. When making an individual portion of a frozen dessert composed of different flavors in different shapes, metal serving dishes are needed so that after assembly the dessert can be placed back in the freezer until ready to serve. These types of stainless steel pedestal sorbet cups are available at nominal cost at restaurant supply stores.

Following are a group of different pezzi duri that may be made with the recipes in this book. I offer them to inspire the food sculptor in you.

⚜

MANNARINA CHINA
(Frozen Stuffed Tangerines)

Take the tangerines to be used for the juice in Sorbettu 'i Clementina and cut off the top to provide an opening in the tangerine about two inches in diameter. Using a small paring knife, carefully remove the flesh from the rind. Work directly over a bowl to catch the juice. Some types of tangerines are loose and easy to remove. If that is not the case, use a spoon to scrape out significant amounts of fruit left behind. Be careful not to break or cut the rind. Match the tops with the hollowed-out rinds and place them in the freezer.

Squeeze the juice out of the fruit by using a food mill fitted with the disk having the smallest holes.

Prepare the sorbet and while it is in the ice cream machine cut aluminum foil in pieces large enough to wrap each tangerine individually.

When the sorbet is ready, fill each rind to overflowing. Place the top piece on as a little hat. The tangerine may be decorated with a pair of large mint leaves to resemble tangerine tree leaves. As each one is filled, wrap it tightly in the foil and freeze.

Remove from the freezer in enough time to allow the sorbet to soften before serving.

⚜

MELUNI 'NGHIACHIATA
(Frozen Melon)

This presentation will work with all types of melons. Choose a melon with an ideal appearance and not too large. Carefully cut out a slice about 1½ inches wide. Using a spoon, scrape out the seedpod and discard. Now scoop out the flesh of the melon. Leave the inside of the melon as smooth as possible. Cut off the melon from the slice and use all of this melon flesh to prepare a granita or sorbet. In all cases except watermelon, additional melon will be needed to compensate for the space of the seedpod. Fill the melon with water from a measuring cup to get a better sense of how much sorbet mixture you will need.

Drain the melon shell and fit the cut piece in place, using masking tape to hold it securely, as the melon shell will deform in freezing and the piece may no longer fit properly. Place the melon shell in the freezer.

A few minutes before the granita or sorbet is ready, remove the melon shell from the freezer. Use a knife dipped in hot water to pry away the cut slice. Fill the shell through the opening. Sprinkle in sliced almonds as the shell is filled to provide the suggestion of melon seeds. With watermelon add chocolate bits.

When the melon is filled, fit the cut piece back in place, wrap the whole melon in aluminum foil, and freeze.

Place it in the refrigerator a half hour before serving. Bring it to the table with the cut side facing you. Cut it in slices, starting with the original slice, and serve.

As an alternative, the melon shell can be stuffed with sorbet other than that of its own fruit. For example, a bright red strawberry sorbet or raspberry spuma stuffed in a cantaloupe shell makes an extraordinary visual delight.

⚜

TORTA 'I CIUCCULATU
(Chocolate Ice "Cake")

Prepare a recipe of Fràguli suttu Spiritu.

Prepare the recipe for chocolate ice (Granita 'i Ciucculatu). While it is freezing, line a 1-quart fancy ring gelatin mold with plastic wrap. Be sure it adheres to all facets of the mold.

When the ice is ready, fill the ring mold with it. Do not leave any gaps. Smooth the top flat, cover with foil, and freeze until hard.

Unmold the ice onto a serving plate that will tolerate being in the freezer. The mold should release easily because of the plastic wrap, but if it does not, apply a dish towel dampened in hot water. Carefully peel away the plastic wrap. Cover the ice and return it to the freezer.

About ten minutes before serving, remove it from the freezer and uncover it. Place the marinated strawberries in the center of the ring and the marinade in a small pitcher.

Serve the chocolate ice cake cut in slices with some strawberries spooned on top, plus a drizzle of the marinade.

⚜

COPPA 'I TRI COLORI
(Three Flavors in a Cup)

Choose metal pedestal sorbet cups for the number of servings required. Prepare enough Granita 'i Ciucculatu mixture to fill each one level.

Cut a tangerine exactly in half. Juice it and remove any loose pulp from the rind. You now have a perfect hemisphere mold. Continue cutting, juicing, and preparing tangerines until there is a half for each serving. Place the rinds in the freezer.

Mix the juice, together with a proportionate amount of the other ingredients, to make a Sorbettu 'i Clementina.

Prepare enough Granita 'i Caffe to fill one level mini-tart tin for each serving.

Process the chocolate ice in an ice cream machine. When it is ready, fill each chilled sorbet dish with it. Be sure the top is flat. Cover each one with foil and freeze until hard.

Process the tangerine sorbet. Meanwhile, line each half tangerine rind with plastic wrap. When the sorbet is ready, fill each rind with it. Be sure the top is flat. Use the plastic wrap overlapping the edges to cover each one. Freeze until hard.

Process the coffee Iie. Meanwhile, find a small cookie sheet or the underside of a cake pan large enough to fit all the mini-tart tins in one layer. Chill the tins and the cookie sheet in the freezer.

When the ice is ready, fill each tin with it and press it facedown onto the cookie sheet. Freeze until it is hard.

The assembly must be done quickly. The tangerine sorbet will easily de-mold because of the plastic wrap. Unwrap it and place it flat-side down against the chocolate. Remove the rind and then the plastic wrap.

Use a spatula to remove the coffee ice in their tins from the cookie sheet. Place tin side down in a shallow bowl with warm water in the bottom. Because these tins are so small they will release the ice quickly. Place one on top of each hemisphere. As each portion is assembled, cover and freeze it.

Twenty minutes before serving, remove the cups from the freezer and uncover them. Carefully decorate each one with a red or green candied cherry and a piece of candied orange rind on a toothpick tipped with colored cellophane.

⚜

BOMBA 'I CREMA 'I GELATU E SORBETTU 'I FRAGULI
(Lemon Ice Cream and Strawberry Sorbet Bombe)

This multiflavored frozen dessert is molded in a high, rounded form. The surface can be decorated or left plain. The process for making these desserts is simple, once one understands the concept. As an example, I have chosen a bombe of lemon ice cream and strawberry sorbet.

Choose a deep stainless steel or plastic bowl which will contain an adequate amount for the number of servings required.

Prepare a Sorbettu 'i Fraguli equal to one-half the volume of the bowl and a Crema 'i Gelatu in the same amount.

Process the sorbet in an ice cream machine. Meanwhile, place the empty dry bowl in the freezer. When the sorbet is ready, line the walls of the bowl with it right up to the top edge. Work quickly, as the sorbet will melt. If it is sliding around too much and you are unable to line the bowl properly, place it in the freezer again until it is a bit harder.

Place aluminum foil over the sorbet to hold it in place and freeze it until it is very hard. At this time, begin to process the crema.

When the crema is ready, remove the foil from the sorbet and place the crema in the center. Make sure the top is flat and even. Cover and freeze overnight.

Several hours before it is to be served, de-mold the bombe by placing it in a sink of warm water. At the moment the bombe is free when the mold is twisted, quickly turn it over onto a serving plate. Cover it well with foil and place it back in the freezer until 10 minutes before serving.

Remove and let it stand out of the freezer. Cut it in slices and serve.

As an alternative, the center could be filled with two flavors, or different flavors can be placed in the mold in layers, so that the bombe would look striped. The possibilities are numerous, the amusement endless.

❧

CASSATA 'I GELATU A SICILIANA
(Sicilian Ice Cream Bombe)

Cassata comes from the word *cassa*, which means "chest" or "bank." Cassata gelatu is certainly the treasure chest of all frozen desserts—a bombe composed of two or more flavors of gelatu, layered with Pan 'i Spagna (Italian spongecake) and spuma, and decorated with spuma, candied fruits, and peels. It is a delight to the eye and an orgy to the taste.

I have found that baking the Pan 'i Spagna two days before the cassata is to be served, and processing the gelatu in the machine, and assembling the cassata the day before, gives it an opportunity to really become hard in the freezer and also gives the flavors a chance to commingle.

Cassata 'i gelatu is formed in a mold called a stampo di gelato. For this recipe, a five-quart bowl with a rounded bottom, about 8½ inches in diameter at the top, and 7 inches deep, works very well. Be sure that the material of your bowl is freezer safe.

FOR 12 TO 16 SERVINGS

1 recipe Gelatu 'i Pistacchiu	1 cup sugar
1 recipe Gelatu 'i Ciucculatu	3 cups cream
1 recipe Pan 'i Spagna	candied fruits, chopped and whole
made with vanilla	⅓ cup chocolate chips
8 egg whites, from eggs used	¼ cup brown rum
in the gelato, refrigerated	sliced almonds
¼ teaspoon powdered eggshell	

Process the pistachio ice cream first. While it is in the machine, slice the Pan 'i Spagna. Cut away two opposite crusts of the Pan 'i Spagna with a serrated bread knife. Cut the cake in slices ¼-inch thick.

Line the bowl with one layer of the cake. Cut and fit pieces so that the entire surface of the bowl is well covered. Because of the curvature of the bowl, the slices may end up in a swirl pattern, which is acceptable.

When the pistachio ice cream is ready, place it in the bottom of the bowl over the Pan 'i Spagna. Make sure there aren't any air pockets. Cover with a layer of Pan 'i Spagna, again fitting pieces. Sprinkle it with rum and place it in the freezer immediately.

Process the chocolate ice cream next. When it is ready, place it on top, followed by another layer of Pan 'i Spagna, and a sprinkle of rum. Again place it in the freezer.

Now it is time to prepare the first batch of spuma. Beat four of the egg whites with ⅛ teaspoon powdered eggshell until they are very stiff but not dry. Sprinkle a small amount of the sugar on top while continuing to beat. When the egg whites have absorbed this sprinkling, add more until ½ cup of sugar is incorporated. This is done in this manner so that the egg whites will not collapse. When it is ready, refrigerate while preparing the whipped cream.

Whip half the cream not too stiff and add all of the chocolate chips, some chopped candied fruits to taste, and sliced almonds.

Fold together with the egg whites and add to the bowl on top of the last layer. Cover with a layer of Pan 'i Spagna and sprinkle with rum. Make sure the top is flat and even, since it will become the bottom when the cassata is unmolded. Cover and freeze overnight. The next morning, prepare the second batch of spuma without any candied fruits or chocolate chips or almonds. Keep it in the refrigerator until the cassata is de-molded.

The only place where the cassata may stick to the bowl is around the top edge. If that is the case, carefully release it with a small knife. Turn it over onto a flat plate or cardboard circle at least one inch larger in diameter. The cassata should release quite easily. Remove the bowl and, working quickly, spread the spuma evenly on the outer surface of the cassata, creating either a smooth or decorative pattern. Place it in the freezer for about ½ hour so that the spuma hardens enough to hold candied fruits and candied peel decorations.

Decorate the cassata in the most garish fashion you can imagine with the candied fruit and peel. Cover it very well with aluminum foil and return it to the freezer.

Ten to fifteen minutes before serving, remove it from the freezer. Slice it using a large knife warmed in hot water.

MENU SUGGESTIONS

$\mathcal{T}$he menus in this section are listed for one week in each season and for holidays. The meals suggested for during the week tend to be simpler and easier to prepare. Overall these menus are designed to show how food goes together to establish a diversity of flavor in the same meal.

Dining is not feeding. Sadly, we in America traditionally have little sense of the concept of being *a tavola,* at the table. The table is a setting where food creates a forum for a group of family or friends to exchange thoughts and feelings and to enjoy the simple pleasure of eating together. When dining alone, one can enjoy the time in reflection or by accompanying the meal with good music. The amount of time set aside for these events can be tailored by what is appropriate or practical.

Perhaps these menus can provide a glimpse into another place and time, a place where men rode horses, women carried parasols, and when they sat down at the table to dine they took the time to enjoy the bountiful riches of the earth and each other's company.

SPRING
Sunday

Insalata 'i Cacuocciuli, Artichoke Salad
Alivi, Olives
Pasta alla Norma, Fresh Pasta With Eggplant
Punta 'i Pettu Chini, Stuffed Breast of Veal
Insalata Mista, Mixed Green Salad
Suppa Inglisi, Meringue Cream Pie

Monday

Pupetteddi 'Nbrudu, Meatball Soup
'a Pizza Fritta, Fried Pizza
Fraguli suttu Spiritu, Strawberries Soaked in Sweet Vermouth

Tuesday

Cavateddi cu Broculi Rabi, Shell Pasta With Italian Broccoli
Rugnuni chi Patati, Kidneys and Potatoes
Torta 'i Ciucculatu, Chocolate Ice "Cake"

Menu Suggestions

Wednesday

Schiachata c'Anciovi, Pizza With Anchovies
'a Frittedda
Biancumanciari, Cornstarch Pudding

Thursday

L'Ova 'Ncamissa, Egg-in-a-Shirt Soup
Pupetti, Meatballs
Insalata Mista, Mixed Green Salad
Biscotti 'i Finucchi, Fennel Seed Cookies

Friday

Risuttu chi Calamari, Risotto With Squid
Cacuocciuli Chini, Stuffed Artichokes
Mannarina China, Frozen Stuffed Tangerines

Saturday

Tagghiarini chi Cacuocciuli, Tagliatelle With Artichokes
Quagghia 'n Pignata, Pan Roasted Quails
Funci Chini, Stuffed Mushrooms
Insalata Mista, Mixed Greek Salad
Coppa 'i Tri Colori, Three Flavors in a Cup

SUMMER

Sunday

Insalata 'i Calamari, Squid Salad
Alivi, Olives
Malfatti Marinara, "Badly Made" Pasta Marinara
Braciola 'i Pisci Spata, Swordfish Rolls
Cippudeddi Auruduci, Sweet and Sour Onions
Insalata Mista, Mixed Green Salad
Bomba 'i Crema 'i Gelatu e Sorbettu 'i Fraguli,
Lemon Ice Cream and Strawberry Sorbet Bombe

Monday

Mirruzzu Sciuscieddu, Poached Whiting
Insalata Mista, Mixed Green Salad
Granita 'i Meluni, Melon Ice

Tuesday

Pasta Marinara, Sailor's-Style Pasta
Cervoluzza, Sausage
'a Scarola, Escarole
Sorbettu 'i Kiwi, Kiwi Sorbet

Wednesday

Capunatina, Eggplant and Olive Salad
Gambereddi cu Mugghiu, Shrimp With "Mugghiu" Sauce
Pumadamuri Verdi 'Ninsalata, Green Tomato Salad
Insalata 'i Patati, Potato Salad
Spuma 'i Lampuni, Raspberry Spuma

Thursday

Pasta 'a Carrittera, Carter's-Style Pasta
Sardi a Beccaficu, Stuffed Fresh Sardines
Insalata Mista, Mixed Green Salad
Granita 'i Limuni, Lemon Ice

Friday

Pasta cu Finucchi, Pasta With Fennel
Tunnina chi Cippuddi, Tuna With Onions
Insalata Mista, Mixed Green Salad
Spuma 'i Ragina Niura, Black Grape Spuma

Saturday

Salami 'i Tunnu 'Nstemperata, Salami of Tuna in Stemperata
Perciateddi chi Pisci Spata, Perciatelli With Swordfish
Spiteddi, Meat Rolls
Insalata Mista, Mixed Green Salad
Gelatu 'i Ficu, Fig Ice Cream

AUTUMN
Sunday

Pipi sutt'Ogghiu, Bell Pepper Salad
Alivi, Olives
Pasta 'Ncaciata, Cheesed Pasta
Agneddu Cartociatu, Leg of Lamb Cooked in Paper
Cippuddi ca Marsala, Onions Marsala
Insalata Mista, Mixed Green Salad
Sfuagghiu, Polizzian Cheese Cake

Monday

Minestra 'i Linticchi, Lentil Soup
Frocia 'i Patati, Sicilian-Style Potato Omelet
Cecilini, Sesame Seed Cookies

Tuesday

Pasta e Piseddi, Pasta With Peas
Ficateddi ca Marsala, Chicken Livers Marsala
Gelatu 'i Ciucculatu, Chocolate Ice Cream

Wednesday

Pipi sutt'Ogghiu, Bell Pepper Salad
Alivi, Olives
Braciola, Sicilian Stuffed Beef Cutlets
Torta 'i Ricotta, Ricotta Pie

Thursday

Pasta Agghiu Ogghiu, Pasta With Garlic and Oil
Cervoluzza, Sausage
i Cucuzzeddi, Zucchini
Gelatu 'i Castagne, Chestnut Ice Cream

Friday

Pasta chi Sardi a Mari, Pasta With Sardines, Still in the Sea
Calamari Chini a Ghiotta, Stuffed Squid, Glutton's style
Insalata Mista, Mixed Green Salad
Gelatu 'i Nucceddi, Hazelnut Ice Cream

Saturday

Pasta ca Cucuzza, Pasta With Sicilian Squash
Gaddina Catanisi, Catania-Style Chicken
Insalata Mista, Mixed Green Salad
Gelatu 'i Pistacchiu, Pistachio Ice Cream

❧

WINTER

Sunday

Capunatina, Eggplant and Olive Salad
Conchigguni Chini, Baked Stuffed Shells
Gaddina Cippudata, Chicken With Smothered Onions
Insalata Mista, Mixed Green Salad
Sfuagghiu, Polizzian Cheesecake

Monday

Brudu 'i Gaddina, Chicken Soup
L'Ova 'Sbatuta, Zabaglione

Tuesday

Risuttu chi Funci, Risotto With Mushrooms
'a Scarola, Escarole
Biancumanciari, Cornstarch Pudding

Wednesday

Pasta ca Muddica e L'Ova, Pasta With Bread Crumbs and Eggs
Insalata Mista, Mixed Green Salad
Biscotti 'i Pan 'i Spagna, Anisette Toast

Menu Suggestions

Thursday

Stincud 'Agneddu Stuffatu, Lamb Shank Stew
Cannola, Cannoli

Friday

Cazziddi, Potato Croquettes
Suppa 'i Pisci, Fish Soup
Aranci e Finucchi 'Ninsalata, Orange and Fennel Salad
Budinu 'i Risu, Rice Pudding

Saturday

Pasta cu Sparaceddu Arriminatu, Pasta With Cauliflower
Pisci Arrustutu chi Cacuocciuli o Finucchi,
Roasted Fish With Artichoke or Fennel
Insalata Mista, Mixed Green Salad
Sfinci Ammilati, Puffs With Honey

❧

EASTER
Cacuocciuli Mandorlata, Artichokes With Almond Sauce
Alivi, Olives
'a Tumala d'Andrea
Coscia 'i Agneddu Arrustutu chi Patati, Roast Leg of Lamb With Potatoes
Funci Chini, Stuffed Mushrooms
Insalata Mista, Mixed Green Salad
Cassata 'i Gelatu a Siciliana
Acceddu cu L'Ova, Easter Cakes

❧

CHRISTMAS DAY
Baccalaru a Ghiotta, Dried Salted Codfish Salad
Alivi, Olives
'a Tumala d'Andrea
Capuni Chini 'i Castagne, Roasted Capon Stuffed With Chestnuts
Carduna Friuta, Fried Cardoons
Cippuddi ca Marsala, Onions Marsala

Aranci e Finucchi 'Ninsalata, Orange and Fennel Salad
Cuciaddatu, Christmas Pastry

⚜

BUFFET FOR NEW YEAR'S EVE
Capunatina, Eggplant and Olive Salad
Pipi Chini a Nana Giambalvo, Nana Giambalvo's Stuffed Peppers
Alivi, Olives
Sardi a Beccaficu, Stuffed Fresh Sardines
Coscia 'i Maiale Arrustutu, Roast Loin of Pork
Aranci e Finucchi 'Ninsalata, Orange and Fennel Salad
Insalata 'i Linticchi, Lentil Salad
Risu 'Ninsalata, Rice Salad
Insalata Mista, Mixed Green Salad
Cuciaddatu, Christmas Pastry (formed in the individual size)
Sfinci Ammilati, Puffs With Honey

⚜

THE FEAST DAY OF ST. AGATHA
(February 5)

Salami 'i Tunnu 'Nstemperata, Salami of Tuna in Stemperata
Maccaruni chi Mulinciani 'a Furnu, Baked Macaroni With Eggplant
Quagghia 'n Pignata, Pan-Roasted Quails
Insalata Mista, Mixed Green Salad
Minni 'i Virgini, Virgins' Breasts

⚜

THE FEAST DAY OF ST. JOSEPH
(March 19)

Torta 'i Cacuocciuli, Artichoke Pie
Pasta chi Sardi d'Andrea, Baked Pasta With Fresh Sardines
Aranci e Finucchi 'Ninsalata, Orange and Fennel Salad
Sfinci 'i San Guiseppi, Filled Puffs

INGREDIENTS

ALMOND MEAL

This coarse ground meal is generally available in health food stores. To make almond meal, if flour grinding equipment is available to you, grind raw unbleached almonds into a coarse meal consistency. If the almonds are ground too fine, your meal will become almond butter and not useful in these recipes.

Store it in a tightly closed container in a cool, dry place.

ANCHOVIES

Use anchovies that are packaged flat in olive oil in two-ounce tins. The best are ones that are dry and firm.

Anchovies are also packed in jars, either in vinegar or salt. These sometimes must be refrigerated. The salted ones must always be washed thoroughly before use.

Always add anchovies that have been melted in a double boiler. Detailed instructions for this process are given with the recipe for Pasta cu Sparaceddu Arriminatu (Pasta With Cauliflower).

BREAD CRUMBS

Always use fine, unflavored bread crumbs made from the crust and white of good Italian bread. To make these, begin by saving the ends of the bread stored uncovered or in a paper bag in a dry place until they are completely dry and hard. They may be crumbed on the fine side of a cheese grater or in a food processor. Stored in a tightly closed container in a cool, dry place, they have a long shelf life.

To toast bread crumbs, place them in a heavy skillet lightly greased with extra virgin olive oil. Set the heat very low. Turn the bread crumbs with a spatula to distribute the oil. At first, nothing will happen, but the bread crumbs will toast quite quickly. Be aware of this and turn them with a spatula to prevent burning. Keep turning and toasting until they are dark brown, but not in any way burned. Remove them immediately from the pan to stop them from toasting further.

CAPERS

Capers are the pickled seeds of a shrub grown in the regions of the Mediterranean. They are graded according to size, the smallest being called nonpareil. I, however, find the larger ones to have more flavor. They are packed in either vinegar or salt. Depending on their use, the vinegar ones may be rinsed before use. The salt-cured ones, which have a subtler flavor, must always be thoroughly rinsed to remove the salt before they are used.

CHEESES

The type and quality of cheese used in these recipes is essential for good results.

Caciocavalo is a cheese similar in texture to provolone, but it is made from pure cow's milk. It is sweeter, less sharp than provolone. It is imported from Sicily. The name caciocavalo means "horse cheese." It is traditionally transported by horse cart; hence, the name.

Provolone is made from a mixture of cow's and sheep's milk. It is suggested as a substitute for caciocavalo, but it is a bit saltier, drier, and sharper. Imported Italian provolone is far superior to any domestic version.

Pecorino is a hard cheese made from sheep's milk. It is white in color, dry, and creamy for its dryness. *Pecorino romano* is a style of pecorino that tends to be milder. *Locatelli* is a brand name of pecorino romano which is the least salty and the mildest of these hard grating cheeses. The name is printed clearly on the wax rind. Domestic romano is available, but it bears no resemblance to the imported product. As is the case with all cheeses, grate these hard cheeses just before use with a hand grater. Generally speaking, machines do not grate cheese, but cut it into tiny round pieces rather than very thin threads.

When purchasing these cheeses, choose a piece which is from the center of the wheel and has the wax rind attached at one end. This wax will help preserve the freshness of the cheese. Store it in a warmer part of the refrigerator tightly wrapped in plastic wrap.

Mozzarella is a first cheese made from sheep's milk, cow's milk, or—the creamiest of all—water buffalo milk. This cheese is called "buffala" mozzarella. Buffala and some other mozzarella are packed in water. These are less salty, moister, and creamier than the type packed dry. This mozzarella packed in water will not string when melted. It is intended to be eaten uncooked. It can, however, be taken out of the water, wrapped in cheesecloth, then in plastic wrap, and left in the refrigerator for a couple of days to dry.

First-quality dry-pack mozzarella is pure white and has more the consistency of cheese than rubber. It is made from whole milk. Mozzarella has a very delicate flavor and always strings when melted rather than turning into a glob.

Ricotta is the second cheese made from the milk of either cows or sheep. After the first cheese is formed, the remaining whey is recooked, "ri-cotta." When it reaches scalding temperature, it is curdled, drained, and lightly salted. This is ricotta.

Because of its freshness and delicacy, it must always be kept refrigerated. As I have stated earlier, it is always better to make your own ricotta from the simple recipe discussed. If it must be store bought, be sure it is pure white in color, creamy, and that the curds are large and do not have a grainy consistency. In addition, be certain it hasn't traveled a long distance. This could suggest that it has been frozen, which destroys it utterly.

Ricotta salata is a salted, pressed, sheep's-milk ricotta, sometimes called hard ricotta or ricotta dura. It is available in two stages of dryness. Both can be grated; the harder, drier version can be grated very fine. There is also a Greek-type of hard ricotta that is called "mizithra." It has a slightly different flavor and texture, but will serve very well.

COFFEE

Sicilians take their coffee short, thick, and strong. To this they add lots of sugar and drink it in one gulp. It is taken after dessert or instead of dessert, but never with it. Cappuccino or espresso with hot milk is drunk only at breakfast.

The best coffee is made in caffé-type espresso machines. At home, the next best method is with a machinetta, the top-of-the-stove espresso maker that is turned over when the water boils. Use the full amount of finely ground espresso coffee and one-half of the water. When the coffee is made, pour a small amount of it with sugar into an espresso cup. Beat it with a fork or whisk until it is frothy and golden. Float a little of this on top of each espresso cup, simulating the gold that is produced by proper espresso machines. This gold froth is called crema.

The custom of serving lemon peel with espresso was conceived in America. The early immigrants could not obtain coffee that was roasted dark and bitter enough for their tastes. They felt that a twist of lemon peel compensated for this.

EGGPLANT

When choosing these in the market, look for ones that are plump, tight, and smooth. They are best when they are the color of their name in French, aubergine. When thumped with a knuckle, they should make a kind of hollow sound.

Always choose eggplants that have an oval or closed line at the blossom end. Those with a round mark where the blossom was will have many more seeds inside.

EGGS

Because of the health problems in this country from eggs produced on large farms, it is always best to buy eggs from small, local farms. Health food stores are a good source for fresh, clean eggs. Many times the carton will be dated and list what the chickens were fed. The best eggs are produced by chickens that are grain-fed and cage-free.

If you shake an egg close to your ear and it is fresh, it will not move around inside the shell. The yolks of fresh eggs when cracked open are high and firm.

The color of the eggshell has no bearing on the taste. It only represents the color and breed of the chicken that laid it. Fertile eggs, however, do have a sweeter, richer flavor.

Before hard-boiling an egg, pierce the shell at the large end with a pin to prevent it from cracking.

GARLIC

There is not a spice which is more maligned and, at the same time, more ill-used than the "stinking rose." As a general rule of thumb, garlic should be used to perfume, not overpower.

The best way to store garlic is in a well-ventilated container in a dark, cool, dry place. Always use garlic directly from the head. Avoid the product that comes refrigerated, peeled, or chopped, as these preparations will compromise the flavor.

GROUND MEATS

In order to control the fat content, quality, and freshness of ground meats, have them specially ground. Choose pork or veal from the shoulder and have it trimmed of all fat before grinding. The only exception to this rule is when the ground meat is to be used for sausage. If the meat is too lean, the sausage will be dry.

HERBS AND SPICES

Unless otherwise stated, the herbs used in the recipes in this book are to be fresh. If dried herbs are substituted, use less, as their flavor is stronger. Always buy them flaked or whole and snap them just before use. Keep dried herbs in a tightly closed container in a cool, dry place. Heat will cause them to lose their flavor quickly.

Follow the same method for spices when this is practical. For example, powdered ginger or cinnamon retain their flavor and are easier to use than whole ginger or cinnamon sticks. Nutmeg should be kept whole and grated before use. Black pepper should always be freshly ground.

MUSHROOMS

Crimini mushrooms, to which are made reference in this book, are a light brown, cultivated mushroom. In years past, they were the type of mushroom commonly found in markets. The white ones we see now are milder in flavor and contain much more liquid.

I have suggested the use of dried mushrooms to augment the flavor of white mushrooms. The best of these are porcini mushrooms. Stored in a tightly closed container, dried porcini mushrooms will last indefinitely. To reconstitute dried mushrooms, place them in a small bowl. Pour boiling water over them, cover, and let them soak for 5 to 10 minutes. Fish the mushrooms out with a fork, leaving behind dirt and small stones. Filter the liquid through a fine mesh strainer before using it.

I do not recommend foraging wild mushrooms unless one is truly expert on the subject. The consumption of even the smallest amount of an inedible mushroom could prove fatal.

If a stronger, wilder mushroom taste is desired, use fresh oyster mushrooms. These are generally available in gourmet markets.

OLIVE OIL

After olives to be pressed for oil are gathered, they are left to dry for a few days. They are then washed and crushed into a paste, seeds and all. The first pressing of this paste will produce an oil with less than 1 percent acidity. It is called extra virgin olive oil. The quality is dependent on the type of olives used; whether or not they were gathered from trees or left to overripen and fall to the ground; the method used for making the paste; and the quantity in which the oil was produced. All of these factors are reflected in the price.

Whenever olive oil is used in the recipes in this book, it is to be extra virgin olive oil. The refined product, called pure olive oil, has had the flavor cooked out of it. Its relative flavor to the olive is the same as corn oil is to corn.

When choosing a bottle or container of extra virgin oil, choose it as you would a bottle of wine. Use the first quality for salads and to dress vegetables, the last for deep frying. The labels, like wine labels, will give the name of the grower, the pressing method, the region the oil is from, and the amount produced. The more specific the label, the better.

Two good regions for fine tasting and well-priced extra virgin olive oil are Southern Italy and Sicily. This oil tends to be fruity, sweet, and rich in olive flavor.

Store olive oil in a dark, cool, dry place. Never refrigerate it. This causes condensation, which will inspire rancidity. An unopened container of extra virgin olive oil will last one year from the time of bottling at the factory. Once it is opened, it has a shelf life, under proper conditions, of two to three months.

It is cost effective to purchase olive oil in large cans. Decant a small amount into an opaque container rather than opening and closing the larger one every time it is used. A clean and dry special wine bottle is excellent for this use.

OLIVES

The olive has been in abundance in Sicily since it was brought there by the ancient Greeks. The mountains of Sicily are dotted with crumbling, Baroque, baronial estates, surrounded by beautifully tended olive groves. The presence of the absentee owners of these estates is noted once a year during the olive harvest. Olives from the tree have a woody bitter flavor and are inedible. In fact, they are slightly toxic. All olives must be cured in some way to make them edible.

Large green and black olives are cured in brine, in order to leach out the bitter acid liquid. At the end of the process they are stored in salt water. These are sometimes called colossal or queen olives. *Oil cured olives* are small black olives cured in salt and packed dry; they resemble small prunes. For the recipes in this book, always use olives with the pits, packed in salt water or oil cured. Pitted olives have no taste. Flavored olives will add flavors not necessarily called for. As has been previously stated, the large olives can be pitted by smashing them with some sort of mallet. Smaller black and green olives can be pitted with a cherry pitter. Oil-cured olives can be pitted by squeezing out the pit.

Olives make a lovely part of an antipasto or a buffet. Italian grocery stores are good sources for olives prepared with olive oil or pickled vegetables. In Sicily, there is a black-brown olive similar to the Greek calamata olive, but slightly smaller. In the countryside, they are put four or five on a small wooden skewer, held over a flame until they turn brown, and served warm.

PANCETTA

Pancetta is Italian bacon. The slab is peppered and rolled and cured with a steam process. It has a milder taste and is leaner than American bacon.

If pancetta cannot be found, the taste can be approximated by blanching slices of American bacon in boiling water for five minutes. Pat them dry and continue with the recipe. Blanching will remove some of the smoky flavor.

PARSLEY

Of the two types of parsley available, the one more suitable for the recipes in this book is called Italian or Armenian parsley. It has flat leaves and a milder, sweeter flavor.

PASTA

Dried pasta is made from 100 percent hard durum wheat or semolina. It will disclose this somewhere on the box. The best pasta is imported from Italy, as it is never gummy and cannot be quickly overcooked. The best of these are from the south or Sicily because of the quality of the water that is used.

Store pasta in a cool, dry place. If long-term storage is required, place the box in a tightly sealed tin.

To cook one or two pounds of pasta, bring 6 quarts of water with two heaping tablespoons of sea salt and two tablespoons of extra virgin olive oil to a boil. The salt will raise the boiling point of the water, helping to prevent the pasta from becoming gummy. The olive oil will keep it from sticking together. When the water boils, drop in the pasta and stir it with a large fork to separate it and keep it from sticking together. Cook it at high heat uncovered, stirring occasionally for 6 to 12 minutes, depending on its size and shape. Pasta is properly cooked when it is *al dente*, which means "to the tooth," that moment when it is completely pliable but still offers slight resistance to the tooth.

Drain the pasta immediately in a colander. Place the colander over the pasta pot for the final shaking and draining. The heat from the pot will aid in keeping the pasta hot. Never add cold water to the pot at the end of its cooking or rinse the pasta, as that will make it cold. In Sicily there are four rush hours a day—the morning, lunch, after siesta, and the end of the workday. In Palermo and other big cities, the most insane of these races is when everyone rushes home for lunch. The reason: God forbid, the pasta should get cold.

The best utensils for tossing pasta are a large ceramic bowl (warmed in hot tap water and dried), a stainless steel pasta rake, and a large stainless steel wok spoon—the type with a metal bowl and handle tipped with wood. A metal rake is strong enough to lift a portion of pasta and the wok tool is large enough to gather pieces from the sauce.

Well-cooked pasta is basic to all pasta dishes. An old Sicilian gesture to show when something is truly delicious is made by holding the index finger against the side of the mouth and turning it back and forth. The gesture implies the toothsome nature of well-cooked pasta.

RICE

Arborio rice is the type of Italian rice most commonly available in this country. It is suitable for all the recipes in this book. Arborio rice is sometimes packaged under the name risotto rice. Be sure, however, that somewhere on the package it says that the contents are arborio rice.

This rice is a short-grained Italian rice high in starch, which accounts for its creamy texture when cooked. It can also tolerate longer cooking, retain a great deal of liquid, and still remain *al dente*. When raw, it's about as long as it is wide and has a little white, pearly dot on one side of the grain.

Arborio rice can be stored in tightly closed containers in a cool, dry place. Unfortunately, it sometimes will attract small grain insects, if stored for a long time.

If arborio rice cannot be obtained locally, it can be easily mail-ordered from a variety of sources.

SAFFRON

Saffron is the dried stigmas of a type of crocus flower. The low yield per flower, in addition to the careful, labor-intensive process of gathering and drying the stigmas, accounts for the high price of this spice. A tiny amount, however, does go a long way.

A product, sold cheaply in large packages, is sometimes called Mexican saffron. This type is inappropriate for the recipes in this book.

SEA SALT

All salt has originated from the sea at one time or other. The product labeled sea salt is taken from sea water rather than from inland salt flats. It has a better "saltier" flavor.

Salt has had a long history of use in food. Before the days of cold storage, it was the primary way of preserving food. That the Roman legions were paid in salt, from which we get the word "salary," is a known historical fact. Today in Italy and Sicily, salt is taxed in the same manner as tobacco and alcohol. Throughout the world it remains the primary flavor enhancer of all cuisines.

Salting food is a matter of personal taste. Its primary purpose, however, is to make food taste more like itself, rather than salty. An excellent method to use in salting food is to smell for it, as tasting could confuse the palate and one could end up with too much salt. To learn this process, bring a small pot of water to a boil. Smell it. Slowly add salt. When you can detect its presence, you have learned the smell of salt. When adding salt to food, this presence is noted when the smell of the food is at its strongest. When preparing soups and sauces, the salt takes longer to develop. Add it in several additions.

In order to reproduce and familiarize yourself with the flow of salt into the food, always use the same shaker or spoon. The hand and the fingertips are the best way to conduct salt, as they are always available for use and completely portable.

Store sea salt in a salt box, near the stove, as the warmth will keep it from sticking together.

TOMATO

The only type of tomato appropriate for tomato sauce is the Italian plum tomato. Most of the year they are available only canned. These cans are labeled "whole and peeled" and are sometimes packed with a basil leaf, which is removed before use.

Some Italian plum tomatoes are grown and packed in California; others in Italy. The Italian product is generally redder, sweeter, softer, and more velvety in texture than the California product. The most desirable type of Italian product is a type of tomato called San Marzano, indicated somewhere on the can. No matter how quaint the label is, or how many Italian words are on the can, examine it carefully to be certain of its origin.

Very often the preparation of tomato sauce in this book requires that tomatoes be passed through a food mill to remove the seeds. This is done to prevent the sauce from gaining a bitter flavor from the seeds. Use the type of food mill that fits over a bowl and has two or three interchangeable disks having differing-sized holes. The holes in the type of mills with only one fixed disk are generally too large. In a pinch, a mesh strainer can be used in conjunction with a thick, round-bottomed cup to push through the tomatoes.

When this process of milling the tomatoes is completed, the only thing left in the top of the mill should be the seeds. It is essential to scrape into the milled tomatoes all of the pulp stuck to the bottom side of the mill.

The recipes calling for fresh Roma or egg-shaped tomatoes can be substituted with other types as long as they are small, sweet, and non-acidic in flavor.

TOMATO PASTE

In the mountains of Sicily during late summer, the countryside is reddened by large boards covered with tomatoes drying in the sun. The resulting sun-dried tomato paste is called *u strattu*. It is placed in containers with olive oil floated on top and used throughout the winter.

When buying tomato paste in little cans in this country, look for Italian products, or the kind that comes in tubes like toothpaste. There is also a sun-dried version in the tube which comes close to the flavor of *u strattu*.

꙳

Following is a short list of mail order sources. Naturally, the more perishable the food item, the less distance it can successfully travel.

FOR IMPORTED ITALIAN AND SICILIAN FOOD ITEMS

Domingo's Italian Grocery
17548 Ventura Boulevard
Encino, California 91316
Telephone: (818) 981-4466

Manganaro's
488 Ninth Avenue
New York, New York 10018
Telephone: (212) 563-5331

Merchant of Vino
29525 Northwestern Highway
Southfield, Michigan 48034
Telephone: (313) 354-6505

FOR RICH, DARK COFFEE

Graffeo Coffee Roasting Company

733 Columbus Avenue

San Francisco, California 94113

Telephone: (415) 986-2420

FOR EXCELLENT ITALIAN COCOA POWDER,

AS WELL AS KITCHEN EQUIPMENT

Williams-Sonoma

317 North Beverly Drive

Beverly Hills, California 90210

Telephone: (310) 274-9127

FOR FOOD MILLS AND OTHER FINE KITCHEN UTENSILS

AND THINGS FOR THE TABLE:

Utensils

210 North Larchmont Boulevard

Los Angeles, California 90004

Telephone: (213) 461-8101

FOR EXQUISITE HAND-PAINTED ITALIAN AND SICILIAN CERAMICS,

INCLUDING SERVING PIECES AND DINNERWARE:

Biordi Art Imports

412 Columbus Avenue

San Francisco, California 94133

Telephone: (415) 392-8096

The Sicilian language is a strong, colorful, and poetic Italianate dialect. It shows the influence of all the cultures that have conquered and colonized the island. The major influences come from the Greek, North African, and Spanish languages.

Unfortunately, the language of Sicily is fast disappearing from the island. It is spoken only in the country and in the home. Until quite recently, no dictionary translated any other language into Sicilian. The only extant dictionaries translated Sicilian into Italian, and they were compiled in the last half of the nineteenth century for people who wished to "better themselves" by learning Italian. Now there are Sicilian-English and English-Sicilian dictionaries. They were written and published by Joseph Bellestri and are available from him at 2819 Yost Boulevard, Ann Arbor, Michigan 48104 Telephone: (313) 971-2170.

The spellings and pronunciations given here are the ones used and spoken in the region of Polizzi Generosa in the Madonie Mountains in the province of Palermo. The Italian words are included for comparison, the English for reference. An asterisk indicates that the Sicilian and the Italian spellings are the same (though the pronunciations may differ).

VOWELS

LETTER	PRONUNCIATION		EXAMPLE
a	ah	as in the a in father	sparaci
	ə	as in sofa, cola	torta
e	e	as in egg, ebb, set	pupetti
i	ee	as in machine	friuta
	i	as in pin	sardi
o	o	as in the first o in Ohio	biscotti
	ô	as in the o of boy, dog	sorbettu
u	u	as in rude, food	lampuni
	yu	as in used, you	agghiu
uo	wo	as in woke	cacuocciuli

CONSONANTS

LETTER	PRONUNCIATION
c	k as in *c*ool, *c*ross, *c*row
	ch as in *ch*oose, moo*ch*, *ch*est
ch	k as in ar*ch*itect
ġ	ġ as in *ġ*ive, *ġ*row
	j as in *ġ*ym, *ġ*esture
ġh	ġ as in *ġh*etto
h	is silent, but is used with c and ġ: *ch*, *ġh*
r	is trilled, as the British might say, "Ve*r*y, ve*r*y"
s	s as in *s*aw, *s*low
	sh as in *sh*ot, *sh*oot
	z as in *z*ip, *z*oo
	zh as in vi*s*ion, deci*s*ion
z	ts as in pi*zz*a

Double Consonants: When these appear within a syllable, or split between syllables, simply double the length of the sound. For example:

pistacchiu [pish-TAHKK-yu]   aġneddu [ah-NYED-du]

In the pronunciation guide, stress is indicated by small capital letters:

chini [KEEN-i]

PRONUNCIATION

SICILIAN	ENGLISH	ITALIAN
acceddu cu l'ova [ah-CHED-du ku LO-və]	Easter cakes	uccello con l'uova
aġneddu cartociatu [ah-NYED-du kahr-to-CHAH-tu]	leg of lamb cooked in paper	aġnello in carta
aranci e finucchi 'ninsalata [ah-RAHN-chi e fin-NU-kyi nin-zah-LAH-tə]	orange and fennel salad	insalata di aranci e finocchio

SICILIAN	ENGLISH	ITALIAN
arancini [ah-rahn-CHEE-ni]	rice balls	*
arrustuciddu 'i aġneddu [ah-RRU-shtu-CHED-du i ah-NYED-du]	lamb shish kabab	arrosticelli di aġnello
babalucci [bah-bah-LU-chi]	snails	lumace
baccalaru a ġhiotta [bah-kah-LAH-ru ah ġee-OT-tə]	dried salted codfish	baccala alla ġhiotta
biancumanciari [be-ahn-ku-mahn-CHYAH-ri]	cornstarch pudding	biancomanġiare
biscotti 'i finucchi [bish-KOT-ti i fin-U-kyi]	fennel-seed cookies	biscotti di finocchio
biscotti 'i pan 'i spaġna [bish-KOT-ti i PAHN-i-SPAHN-yə]	anisette toast	biscotti di pan di spaġna
bomba 'i crema 'i ġelatu **e sorbettu 'i fraġuli** [BOM-bə i KRE-mə i je-LAH-tu e sôr-BET-tu i FRAH-ġu li]	lemon ice cream and strawberry sorbet	bombe di crema di ġelato e sorbetto di fragole
braciola [brah-chi-O-lə]	Sicilian stuffed beef cutlets	involtini di manzo
braciola 'i pisci spata [brah-chi-O-lə i PI-shi SHPAH-tə]	swordfish rolls	involtini di pesce spada
brudu 'i ġaddina [BRU-du i ġahd-DEE-nə]	chicken soup	brodo di ġallina
budinu 'i risu [bu-DEE-nu i REE-zu]	rice pudding	budino di riso
cacuociuli chini [kah-KWO-chi-u-li KEEN-i]	stuffed artichoke	carciofi repiene

SICILIAN	ENGLISH	ITALIAN
cacuocciuli mandorlata [kah-KWO-chi-u-li mahn-dôr-LAH-tə]	artichodes with almond sauce	carciofi con crema di mandorla
calamari chini a ghiotta [kah-lə-MAH-ri KEEN i ah jee-OT-tə]	stuffed squid glutton's style	calamari repinene alla ghiotta
cannola [kah-NNO-lə]	cannoli	cannoli
capuni chini 'i castagne [kah-PU-ni KEEN-i i kahsh-TAH-nye]	roasted capon stuffed with chestnuts	cappone repiene con castagne
capunatina [kah-pu-nah-TEE-nə]	eggplant and olive salad	caponatina
carduna friuta [kahr-DU-nə free-U-tə]	fried cardoons	cardi fritti
cassata 'i gelatu a siciliana [kah-SSAH-tə i je-LAH-tu ah si-chi-LYAH-nə]	Sicilian ice cream bombe	cassata di gelato alla siciliana
cavateddi cu broculi rabi [kah-vah-TED-di ku BRO-ku-li RAH-bi]	shell pasta with Italian broccoli	cavatelli con rapini
cazziddi [kah-TSEED-di]	potato croquettes	crochette di patate
cecilini [che-chi-LEE-ni]	sesame-seed cookies	biscotti di sesami
cervoluzza [cher-vo-LU-tsə]	sausage	salsicce alla siciliana
cippuddi ca marsala [chi-PPUD-di kah mahr-SAH-lə]	onions marsala	cipolle alla marsala

SICILIAN	ENGLISH	ITALIAN
cippudeddi auruduci [chi-ppu-DE-ddi ah-u-ru-DU-chi]	sweet and sour onions	capolline agrodolce
conchigguni chini [kon-chi-GGYU-ni KEEN-i]	baked stuffed shells	conchiglione repiene
coppa i tri colori [KOP-pə i tri ko-LO-ri]	three flavors in a cup	coppa de tre colore
coscia 'i agneddu arrustutu chi patati [KO-shə i ah-NYED-du ahr-ru-SHTU-tu kee pah-TAH-ti]	roast leg of lamb with potatoes	arrosto di coscia di agnello e patate
coscia 'i maiali arrustutu [KO-shə i mah-YAH-li ahr-ru-SHTU-tu]	roast loin of pork	arrosto di maiale
crema 'i gelatu [KRE-mah i je-LAH-tu]	creme anglaise based ice cream	crema di gelato
cucciddatu [ku-chi-DDAH-tu]	Christmas pastry	buccellato
i cucuzzeddi [i ku-ku-TSED-di]	zucchini	i zucchini
i cuduruna [i ku-du-RU-nə]	no English translation	frittelle
ficateddi ca marsala [fee-kah-TED-di kah mahr-SAH-lə]	chicken livers marsala	fagato di pollo alla marsala
fraguli suttu spiritu [FRAH-gu-li SUT-tu SHPI-ri-tu]	strawberries soaked in sweet vermouth	fragole sotto spiritu
'a frittedda [ah frit-TED-də]	no English translation	la frittella

SICILIAN	ENGLISH	ITALIAN
frocia 'i cippuddi [FRO-zhə i chi-PPUD-di]	Sicilian-style onion omelet	frittata di cipolle
frocia 'i patati [FRO-zhə i pah-TAH-ti]	Sicilian-style potato omelet	frittata di patati
frocia 'i sparaci [FRO-zhə i shpah-RAH-chi]	Sicilian-style asparagus omelet	frittata di asparaġi
funci chini [FUN-chi KEEN-i]	stuffed mushrooms	funġhi repiene
ġaddina catanisi [ġah-DDEE-nə kah-tah-NI-zi]	Catania-style chicken	ġallina alla catanese
ġaddina cippudata [ġah-DDEE-nə chi-ppu-DAH-tə]	chicken with smothered onions	ġallina con cipolle
ġambereddi cu muġġhiu [ġahm-be-RED-di ku MUG-ġyu]	shrimp with "muġġhiu" sauce	ġambaretti con salmariġlio
ġelatu 'i castaġne [je-LAH-tu i kah-SHTAH-nye]	chestnut ice cream	ġelato di castaġne
ġelatu 'i ficu [je-LAH-tu i FEE-ku]	fig ice cream	ġelato di fici
ġelatu 'i nucceddi [je-LAH-tu i nu-CHED-di]	hazelnut ice cream	ġelato di nocciole
ġelatu 'i pistacchiu [je-LAH-tu i pish-TAHKK-yu]	pistachio ice cream	ġelato di pistacchio
ġelatu 'i ciucculatu [je-LAH-tu i chyu-kku-LAH-tu]	chocolate ice cream	ġelato a cioccalato
ġranita 'i anġuria [ġrah-NEE-tə i ahn-GU-rree-ə]	watermelon ice	ġranita di anġuria
ġranita 'i ciucculatu [ġrah-NEE-tə chu-kku-LAH-tu]	chocolate ice	ġranita di cioccolato

SICILIAN	ENGLISH	ITALIAN
ġranita 'i limuni [ġrah-NEE-tə i li-MUN-i]	lemon ice	ġranita di limone
ġranita 'i meluni [ġrah-NEE-tə i me-LUN-i]	melon ice	ġranita di melone
ġranita 'i caffe [ġrah-NEE-tə i kah-FFE]	coffee ice	ġranita al caffe
i sproġġhiu pitittu [ee SHPROG-ġyu pi-TEET-tu]	antipasti	ġli antipasti
insalata 'i cacuocciuli [in-zah-LAH-tə i kah-KWO-chi-u-li]	artichoke salad	insalata di carciofi
insalata 'i calamari [in-zah-LAH-tə i kah-lə-MAH-ri]	squid salad	insalata di calamari
insalata 'i linticchi [in-zah-LAH-tə i lin-TEEKK-yi]	lentil salad	insalata di lenticchie
insalata 'i patati [in-zah-LAH-tə i pah-TAH-ti]	potato salad	insalata di patate
insalata mista [in-zah-LAH-tə MEE-shtah]	mixed green salad	*
l'ova 'ncamissa [LO-vah nkah-MEEZ-zə]	egg-in-a-shirt soup	l'uova in camicia
l'ova 'sbatuta [LO-vah shbah-TU-tə]	zabaġlione	zabaġlione
l'ova bruduchiddu [LO-vah bru-du-CHID-du]	egg in a light broth	l'uova in brodo
maccaruni 'a furnu [mah-kkah-RU-ni ah FUR-nu]	baked macaroni	maccheroni al forno

SICILIAN	ENGLISH	ITALIAN
maccaruni chi mulinciani 'a furnu [mah-kkah-RU-ni kee mu-lin-CHYAK-ni ah FUR-nu]	baked macaroni with eggplant	maccheroni con melanzane al forno
malfatti marinara [mahl-FAHT-ti mah-ri-NAH-rə]	"badly made" pasta marinara	malfatti alla marinara
mannarina china [mahn-nah-REE-nah KEEN-ə]	frozen stuffed tangerines	mandorini repiene
meluni 'nghiachiata [me-LUN-i ngyah-CHYAH-tə]	frozen melon	melone ghiacciato
minestra 'i linticchi [mi-NESH-trə i lin-TEEKK-yi]	lentil soup	minestra di lenticchie
minni 'i virgini [MEEN-ni i VIR-jee-ni]	virgins' breast	seni di virgine
mirruzzu sciuscieddu [mi-RRU-tsu zhyu-zhi-ED-du]	poached whiting	merlango in umido
mulinciani a palmigiana [mul-lin-CHYAHN-i ah pahl-mee-JYAHN-ə]	eggplant palmigiana	melanzane all palmigiana
pan 'i spagna [pahn i SHPAHN-yə]	sponge cake	pan di spagna
pani 'i casa [PAH-ni i KAH-zə]	semolina bread	pane di grano duro
pasta 'a carrittera [PAHSH-tə ah kah-rri-TTER-ə]	carter's-style pasta	pasta alla carrettiera
pasta 'ncaciata [PAHSH-tə nkah-CHYAH-tə]	cheesed pasta	pasta infornato con formaggio
pasta agghiu ogghiu [PAHSH-tə AHGG-yu OGG-yu]	pasta with garlic and oil	pasta con aglio e olio

SICILIAN	ENGLISH	ITALIAN
pasta alla norma [PAHSH-tə ahl-lah NOR-mə]	fresh pasta with eggplant	*
pasta ca cucuzza [PAHSH-tə kah ku-KU-tsə]	pasta with Sicilian squash	pasta con melopopone siciliane
pasta ca muddica e l'ova [PAHSH-tə kah mu-DDEEK-ə e LO vah]	pasta with bread crumbs and eggs	pasta con mollica e l'uova
pasta chi sardi a mari [PAHSH-tə kee ZAHR-di ah MAH ri]	pasta with sardines, still in the sea	pasta con le sardi a il mare
pasta chi sardi d'Andrea [PAHSH-tə kee ZAHR-di dahn-DRE-ə]	baked pasta with fresh sardines	pasta con le sardi al'Andrea
pasta cu finucchi [PAHSH-tə ku fi-NU-kyi]	pasta with fennel	pasta con finnocchio
pasta cu sparaceddu arriminatu [PAHSH-tə ku shpah-rah-CHED-du ah-rri-mi-NAH-tu]	pasta with cauliflower	pasta con crema di cavalfiore
pasta e piseddi [PAHSH-tə e pi-ZED-di]	pasta with peas	pasta e piselli
pasta frisca [PAHSH-tə FREESH-kah]	homemade pasta	pasta fresca
pasta friuta [PAHSH-tə free-U-tə]	fried pasta	pasta fritta
pasta marinara [PAHSH-tə mah-ri-NAH-rə]	sailor's-style pasta	pasta alla marinara
perciateddi chi pisci spata [per-chyah-TED-di kee PI-shi SHPAH-tə]	perciatelli with swordfish	perciatelli con pesce spada

SICILIAN	ENGLISH	ITALIAN
pipi chini a Nana Giambolvo [PI-pi KEEN-i ah NAH-nə jyahm-BAHL-vo]	Nana Giambolvo's stuffed peppers	peperoni repiene alla Nonna Giambalvo
pipi sutt'oġġhiu [PI-pi sut-ÔGG-yu]	bell pepper salad	peperoni sott'olio
pisci arrustutu chi cacuocciuli o finucchi [PI-shi ahr-ru-SHTU-tu kee kah-KWO-chi-u-li o fin-nu-kyi]	roasted fish with artichoke or fennel	arrosto di pesce con carciofi o finocchio
'a pizza fritta [ah PEE-tsə freet-tə]	fried pizza	la pizza fritta
pumadamuri verdi 'ninsalata [pu-mah-dah-MUR-i VER-di nin-zah-LAH-tə]	green tomato salad	insalata di pomodori verdi
punta 'i pettu chini [PUN-tə i PET-tu KEE-ni]	stuffed breast of veal	punta di petto repiene
pupetteddi 'nbrudu [pu-pe-TTED-di NBRU-du]	meatball soup	brodo di polpettine
pupetti [pu-PET-ti]	meatballs	polpette
quaġġhia 'n piġnata [KUAHG-ġyə n pin-YAH-tə]	pan-roasted quail	quaglie in padilla
risu 'ninsalata [REEZ-u nin-zah-LAH-tə]	rice salad	insalata di riso
risu pilau [REEZ u PI-lah-u]	rice pilaf	riso pilau
risuttu chi calamari [riz-UT-tu kee kah-lə-MAH-ri]	risotto with squid	risotto con calamari
risuttu chi funci [riz-UT-tu kee FUN-chi]	risotto with mushrooms	risotto con funghi

SICILIAN	ENGLISH	ITALIAN
ruġnuni chi patati [ru-NYU-ni kee pah-TAH-ti]	kidneys and potatoes	roġnone con patate
salami 'i tunnu 'nstemperata [zah-LAH-mi i TUN-nu n-shtem-e-RAH-tə]	salami of tuna in stemperata	salame di tonno in stemperata
sardi a beccaficu [ZAHR-di ah bek-kah-FEE-ku]	stuffed fresh sardines	sarde a beccafico
sardo a cammineddu [ZAHR-di ah kah-mmee-NED-du]	fire-roasted sardines	sarde alla camminetto
'a scarola [ah-shkah-ROL-ə]	escarole	la scarola
schiachata c'anciovi [shkyah-CHAH-tə kahn-CHYO-vi]	pizza with anchovies	pizza con acciughe
sfinci 'i San Guiseppi [SHFEEN-chi i zahn jyu-ZEP-pi]	filled puffs	frittelle di San Guiseppe
sfinci ammilati [SHFEEN-chi ahm-mi-LAH-ti]	puffs with honey	fritelle con miele
sfinciuni cunzatu cu brocculeddu e ricotta [shfin-CHYU-ni kun-TSAH-tu ku bro-kku-LE-ddu e ri-KOT-tə]	sfinciuni filled with broccoli and ricotta	sfincioni con broccoletti e ricotta
sfinciuni cunzatu cu carni e cacciu [shfin-CHYU-ni kun-TSAH-tu ku kahr-ni e KAH-chyu]	sfiniuni filled with meat and cheese	sfincioni con carne e formaggio
sfuagġhiu [shfu-AHG-ġyu]	Polizzian cheesecake	sfoglio
sorbettu 'i fraguli [sôr-BET-tu i FRAH-ġu-li]	strawberry sorbet	sorbetto di fragole
sorbettu 'i kiwi [sôr-BET-tu i kee-WEE]	kiwi sorbet	sorbetto di kiwi

SICILIAN	ENGLISH	ITALIAN
sorbettu i clementina [sôr-BET-tu i kle-men-TEE-nə]	tangerine sorbet	sorbetto di clementine
spiteddi [shpi-TED-di]	meat rolls	spiedini
spuma 'i lampuni [SHPU-mə i lahm-PU-ni]	raspberry spuma	spuma di lampone
spuma 'i ragina niura [SHPU-mə i rah-JEE-nah NE-urə]	black grape spuma	spuma di l'uva nera
stincu d'agneddu stuffatu [SHTIN-ku dah-NYED-du shtu-FFAH-tu]	lamb shank stew	stuffato di stinco d'agnello
suppa inglisi [ZUP-pə in-GLI-zi]	meringue cream pie	zuppa inglese
suppa 'i pisci [ZUP-pə i PI-shi]	fish soup	zuppa di pesce
tagghiarini ca sarsa frisca [tah-ggyah-REE-ni kah ZAHR-zə FREE-shkə]	tagliatelle with fresh tomato sauce	tagliatelle con la salsa di pomadori freschi
tagghiarini chi cacuocciuli [tah-ggyah-REE-ni kee kah-KWO-chi-u-li]	tagliatelle with artichokes	tagliatelle con carciofi
torta 'i cacuocciuli [TÔR-tə i kah-KWO-chi-u-li]	artichoke pie	torta di carciofi
torta 'i ciucculatu [TÔR-tə i chyu-kku-LAH-tu]	chocolate ice "cake"	torta di granita di cioccolato
torta 'i ricotta [TÔR-tə i ri KOT-tə]	ricotta pie	torta di ricotta
'a tumala d'Andrea [ah-tu-MAH-lə dahn-DRE-ə]	rice bombe	bomba di riso e pasta al'Andrea
tunnina chi cippuddi [tu-NNEE-nə kee chi-PPUD-di]	tuna with onions	tonno con cipolle

ACKNOWLEDGMENTS

$\mathscr{I}$ wish to extend my sincerest thanks and appreciation to my mother, Kate, and my aunts, Mae Coco and Josephine Coco, for their exquisite memories of people, dates, places, and food; my cousin Frances Vilardi MacEwen, for reminding me of the beauty and richness of our Sicilian heritage; my cousins Sofia Placa Kaprowski and Philip Vilardi, for their input on Sfuagghiu and snails; David Nuell, Michael Lewis, and Gary Quinn, for their support and involvement with this project; and Becky Sue Epstein, for her incomparable proposal outline; Elinor La Fontaine, whose careful and thoughtful word processing turned recordings of my handwritten manuscript into a legible presentation; my publisher, Steven Schragis, a gentleman who successfully walks the line between altruism and commerce; and especially to my lovely wife, Carol, whose playful nickname for me, "Monsieur le Menu," expresses her support for and her patience with my delicious obsession.

ABOUT THE AUTHOR

$\mathcal{V}$incent Schiavelli was born and raised in Brooklyn. He attended New York University's Tisch School of the Arts in the late sixties, where he studied acting. For the past twenty-three years he has pursued a career as an actor, appearing in character roles in over one hundred films and televsion shows. Most notable are his roles in *One Flew Over the Cuckoo's Nest*, *Amadeus*, *Fast Times at Ridgemont High*, *Batman Returns*, and *Ghost*.

Mr. Schiavelli lives in Los Angeles with his wife, Carol Mukhalian, an international concert harpist. Part of the time Andrea, his six-year-old son from a previous marriage, lives with them. "Papa" looks forward to teaching Andrea about cooking when he is tall enough to reach the stove.

INDEX